# ORVIS GUIDE
## TO BEGINNING FLY TYING

# ORVIS GUIDE
# TO BEGINNING FLY TYING

ERIC LEISER & MATT VINCIGUERRA

ABENAKI Publishers, Inc.
P.O. Box 4100
Bennington, VT 05201

Cover design by Larry Largay
Production/Layout: Michelle Thorpe

Third printing 1994
ISBN 0-936644-16-8

# CONTENTS

1 GETTING STARTED
   Things You Should Know                                      7

2 WOOLLY BUGGER
   An Ideal Beginner's Fly                                    14

3 DARK HENDRICKSON NYMPH
   A Foundation in Nymph Tying                                25

4 GOLD-RIBBED HARE'S EAR NYMPH
   An All-Purpose Subsurface Fly                              32

5 LEADWING COACHMAN
   A Classic Wet Fly                                          39

6 BLACK-NOSE DACE AND BLACK & WHITE MARABOU
   Two Popular Baitfish Patterns                              46

7 DARK HENDRICKSON DRY FLY
   A Model for Many Mayflies                                  55


BIBLIOGRAPHY                                                  67

GLOSSARY                                                      70

# 1 GETTING STARTED
## Things You Should Know

THE BEGINNING SECTION of a book is usually entitled the Introduction, Foreword, or Preface. Although these few pages are important to the subject matter, most readers skip them, preferring to get to the heart of the book. In this instance, however, the following words will be more important to you than to me hence the oblique heading which I hope has attracted your attention.

The purpose of this book is to introduce you to the craft of tying flies for fishing; to get you started in one of the most enjoyable and creative hobbies related to the sport of angling; to show you what you will need in the way of tools and how to select materials; but most of all, to lead you down the easiest path while you learn tying techniques and procedures.

Fly tying is not complicated or difficult, nor is it a mysterious art form that takes years to master. Once you begin your first lesson, in a matter of minutes you will be able to tie a fly that will catch fish. After all, fly tying is nothing more than lashing and securing a few materials, feathers, fur, or other natural or synthetic

fibers to the shank of a hook. Upon completion these materials will resemble an aquatic or terrestrial insect, baitfish, or an impressionistic rendition of something on which trout and other fish feed.

As with any new endeavor, your first attempts at working with thread, hooks, and materials may feel a little awkward and you'll have to proceed slowly. It's like learning to ride a bike, play the piano, or hit a baseball –the muscles required to perform the activity have not as yet learned to do what your mind tells them. Yet, with practice, everything falls into place. So it is with fly tying. Your fingers must first become educated and accustomed to certain movements before they can function with fluidity and speed. As you proceed you will find that each succeeding fly will be better than the first. Learning to tie flies is similar to learning how to ride a bike. Once you have the hang of it, which will occur in a fairly short time, you will never forget how to do it. Dexterity and expertise come with practice, and the more you practice, the quicker you will reach that first plateau.

The fly patterns represented in this book are but a handful of many thousands that exist. However, they have been carefully selected for three reasons:

1. They are representative of many other patterns, so once you learn to tie these flies you will be able to tie other similar types that use the same procedures.

2. They are relatively easy to construct.

3. They are highly effective fishing flies and among the most widely used by anglers.

## IMPORTANT!

What you learn in these pages will be invaluable in setting you on your way to becoming a proficient fly tier. Nevertheless, as in most things and especially in hobbies and sports, the printed word can only take you so far. No book, publication, or even video, no words or photographs can replace the firsthand experience of having someone teach you in person, or at least observing another fly tier at work. You will learn more quickly and gain knowledge rapidly by attending fly-tying classes. When it's coupled with personalized, visual instruction, the printed word will have more meaning. Fortunately, today there are quite a number of fly-tying classes or schools conducted by local chapters of Trout Unlimited (TU) and the Federation of Fly Fishers (FFF). A list of organizations is included at the back of this book. Many fly and tackle shops also offer tying classes. Fees are usually reasonable and, in some cases with TU or FFF chapters, may only involve membership dues. If at all possible, attend them.

When you progress to a point where you are comfortable with your tying, you should acquire a few books for additional information. Check the bibliography for further details.

## HOW TO USE THIS BOOK

Because this is a basic manual (as basic as the ABC's when you learned to read and write) I suggest you tie the flies in the order presented. Don't skip around simply because your interest lies only in a particular category of flies. For example, if your inclination is to fish only dry flies, nymphs, or other fly pattern types, don't ignore the procedures in other sections. This manual is written as a progressive experience in showing methods and techniques which will eventually be useful for tying all types of flies and often you will be referred to earlier procedures as you progress.

By starting at the beginning, and advancing only when you have mastered the contents of each page, you will learn the meaning of fly-tying terms and a little about each material as you proceed. When a material or term is mentioned in succeeding pages you will have already become acquainted with it.

If, after you have completed this course, you wish to check the meaning of a term or word, or wish to know something more about a material or pattern, there is a glossary at the back to assist you.

## BEFORE WE BEGIN

In addition to materials and hooks, there are tools and equipment you will need before you can produce your first fly. You may already have a vise, a pair of scissors, and perhaps some odds and ends which you've picked up on a whim, or that someone has given to you. Whether you have equipment or not, you will do well to read the following recommendations.

## FLY-TYING KITS

As a general rule I don't recommend fly-tying kits. There are, however, some exceptions, the most notable of which would be one in which the materials and tools are prepared by fly-fishing specialists.

The kits you want to avoid are those which contain inferior tools and an array of brightly colored feathers and furs which will be of little use during the learning process; or, if the materials have no relation to the flies being tied in whatever instruction booklet is enclosed. Most reputable dealers no longer sell these inexpensive kits since they only discourage beginners and are bad for business. Should you decide to begin by buying a kit, there are a few guidelines you can follow.

1. Make sure that the tools are of good quality and serve the purpose. (A list of recommended tools follows.) Some dealers offer the option of a kit with or without certain tools, or a kit in which the selection of a vise may be upgraded. If a kit has the proper materials and you have the option to improve on your selection of tools, it is worth considering.

2. Check the instruction booklet that comes with the kit and ascertain what patterns you will be tying. Then

check the materials, hooks, and threads in the kit to see if they relate to the patterns listed.

## TOOLS

After you've been tying for a period of time you'll acquire a number of tools and gadgets which you'll enjoy working with, even though they may not be absolutely necessary. For now, we are going to list certain basic tools that you will need and use as long as you pursue this hobby.

### Vises

There are many types of vises on the market ranging in price from under $20 to over $200. Buy the best you can afford. However, a very good vise can be obtained at the lower end of the price range. Your primary concern should not be price but performance. Here are the things you want to look for.

1. Make sure the jaws hold a hook securely. Except for the very large hooks (1/0 and larger) you should be able to press down on a hook shank with your thumb and bend the hook. If it slips with thumb pressure it will slip while you are tying. Most fly shops will allow you to inspect a vise for this attribute.

2. The vise should be capable of holding a range of hook sizes, preferably from a size 1/0 down to a tiny 24. Some manufacturers offer interchangeable jaws for extra-small or extra-large hooks. For a novice, most tying will be on hook sizes from 6 to 14.

3. The barrel of the vise should be tilted or be capable of being tilted to a thirty to forty-five degree angle. Don't buy a vise that stays in a fixed horizontal position.

4. Try to obtain a vise that uses a lever mechanism. It is easy to use and won't form callouses on your thumb and finger.

5. It is preferable to use a vise that is adjustable for height. C-clamp vises are height adjustable. I do much of my own tying with a pedestal (or base type) vise because I am occasionally called upon to do demonstrations in places other than my home. Whichever type of vise you choose you should either adjust the vise, chair, or table so that your hands will comfortably fall to the head of the vise in front of you. (The vise in the photographic sequences is no longer available. I've tied with it in memory of its designer, Peter Phelps, who was a close friend.)

### Hackle Pliers

This tool is primarily designed to hold a hackle (a feather) by the tip while it is being wound around the hook shank to form the collar on a dry or wet fly. There should be enough tension between the jaws of the pliers so that the feather does not slip from its grasp while being wound. Nor should there be any sharp edges on the jaws which will inadvertently cut the feather. Here is a test you can make before buying hackle pliers: Place the tips of a small feather between the jaws; hold the feather between the thumb and fingers of one hand and the pliers in the other and pull them apart. The feather should break rather than slip from the jaws.

### Bobbin

This tool holds a spool of thread. There are various types, and selection of one type over another is a matter of personal preference. Whichever type you decide to use, make sure that the bobbin controls the thread under smooth, even tension. You should be able to pull the thread through the bobbin tube without breaking the thread, yet the tension should not be so light that it unwinds by itself during a tying procedure.

Always check the bobbin tube at both ends to make sure there are no burrs or sharp edges that may cut the thread.

## Scissors

The requisites here are sharp blades, fine points, and finger holes large enough to accommodate your own hand. Many years ago, fly tiers used their mother's embroidery scissors, since these were designed for very fine work. Most soon found that the finger holes on embroidery scissors were much too small. Those who could afford to bought surgeon's scissors. Today we have available to us a variety of scissors with large finger holes in price ranges from $5 to $75 .

When purchasing a pair of scissors check them by taking a piece of feather, fluff, or thread and cutting the very end or tip of the material with the tips of the scissors. If the particular fiber severs easily and is not pushed forward when the blades mesh, the scissors are sharp.

## Dubbing Needle

This is simply a sewing needle or pin, held in a piece of wood, plastic, or metal. It is used to apply a drop of head cement to the thread windings of completed flies and to poke out fibers trapped under thread windings. It can also be used to roughen the bodies of nymphs. (You'll see it used in this manner on one of our flies, the Gold-ribbed Hare's Ear nymph, in a later section.)

While there are a number of these inexpensive needles on the market, the one I recommend is the Matarelli type since it is formed with a shepherd's crook at one end. This crook, sort of a U-shape curve, can be used with a doubled loop of thread for one of the dubbing methods employed when forming bodies using coarse furs. (You'll see this method later.)

## Tweezers

What you don't need here, contrary to popular belief, are tweezers with sharp points. You want the kind that are square or rounded at the tips. These can be purchased inexpensively at a drug store or supermarket. Though you'll find them handy for picking up hooks and bits of material, the primary function will be to help you align, to measure, and easi-

ly hold in position certain materials during the construction of wings on dry and wet flies.

## Whip Finisher

I don't recommend using this tool during the learning process because I want you to understand the principle of the whip-finish knot, and how to form it with your fingers.

Once you have mastered this knot and you have a few hours of experience in fly tying, learning to use the whip-finish tool will make things much easier and faster. It is a particular boon for those of you who have rough hands which tend to fray fine thread.

There are several whip finishers on the market but my preference is the Matarelli design, since it allows you to place your turns of thread exactly where you want them.

## Emery Board, Pumice Stone, Nail Clipper, Hand Cream

These items will not be used in fly tying. Some of you may never need them, but many of us find them useful for keeping our fingers smooth and free of rough skin and nails which may catch the tying thread and possibly get in the way of other operations. You'll soon know if you need one or more of these.

## NECESSITIES

In addition to your tools, you will need certain items that will make lashing the materials to the hook shank just a little easier. Try to become familiar with them before making a purchase.

### Threads

The ideal in fly tying is to use the finest thread available to tie and secure your materials to a hook shank. As a beginner, however, you may find the commonly used size 6/0 thread just a bit too weak for your inexperienced fingers. If this presents a problem, step up to the next largest diameter (either 3/0 or 4/0) until you get used to handling threads. Fine threads make for a neater fly because they keep bulkiness to a minimum. Therefore, the quicker you get used to fine thread, the sooner your flies will improve in appearance.

Thread sizes are designated by the number of zeros listed on the label; the more zeros the finer the diameter. Thus, a size 000000 is of a smaller diameter than a size 0000. Because it is a little impractical to print so many zeros on a small label, manufacturers have simply preceded the zero numerically to indicate size. For example, a listed 6/0 size is equal to six zeros. When threads reach diameters larger than a single zero they are designated with letters of the alphabet in which size A is the finest and an increase in size is related to B, C, D and so forth. Fly tiers rarely use sizes larger than A, while fishermen who build their own rods generally wrap guides with a size up to D.

### Wax

You may wish to purchase a tube of tacky wax even though some threads are pre-waxed. As a beginner your fingers may not be accustomed to applying the proper pressure to fur and thread when forming a dubbed-fur body, and a little additional wax on the thread will make things easier. The types I prefer are those which come in a retractable tube-type container. You can apply the wax to the tying thread without getting your fingers gooey or sticky.

### Head Cements and Lacquers

Head cement, or head lacquer, is a clear substance, and is used to coat the thread windings after a fly has been completed or to create other tacky, non-slip situations. Clear nail polish can be used in its place.

Colored lacquers, in black, red, yellow, and other colors, are used to paint the heads of streamer, salmon and saltwater flies. Occasionally, two, and sometimes three, colors are used to represent the pupil and iris of the eyes on the head.

### Hooks

There are hundreds of styles of hooks, in sizes ranging from a tiny 32 (barely ⅛ inch in total length) to gaff-like monsters used for sharks. In fly tying we need to be concerned with only a limited variety of types and sizes. The largest hook used in fly tying is a size 5/0 which requires a fairly stout rod to cast but is a necessity when fishing for tarpon or other gamefish in the 100-pound class. The smallest hook commonly used is a size 26 and it is also needed for those times when trout are feeding on the tiniest of mayflies called Tricorythodes and only an imitation tied in the proper size, shape, and color will take them. For most of us, however, our tying usually will be done on hooks ranging in size from 4 to 18.

Hook sizes are designated in the following manner. Hooks smaller than a size 1 climb a numerical ladder in even sizes from 2 to 32. So, a size 4 is smaller than a 2 and a size 14 is smaller than a 12. Hooks which are larger than size 1 progress numerically in the opposite direction but have a slash (/) and a zero (0) added after the number. Thus, size 3/0 is larger than a size 2/0 and so forth.

Hooks also come in various shapes, that is, that portion which curves from the end of the shank to eventually terminate in the barb and point. The three most common shapes of hooks used for fly tying are the Model Perfect, which is used more than the others; the Limerick; and the Sproat. Don't be overly concerned about hook shapes at this time.

Light-wire hooks are used for dry flies to help keep the fly afloat, and heavy-wire hooks are used for subsurface patterns so they sink more rapidly. Hooks that are longer in length are used for baitfish imitations. Hooks are manufactured for specific purposes, and the manufacturers often indicate such usage on their labels. In addition to the model number and size of the hook, you may see the letters XL, which means that the hook is extra long. Differing lengths are labeled 3XL, 4XL, or 6XL, and of the three, 6XL is the longest. Unfortunately, there is no industry standardization and an XL hook of a size of one manufacturer may not be exactly as long as that of another. Hooks may also be marked XF which means extra-fine wire, or 3XF (extra, extra, extra fine) or XS (extra short). Again, don't be overly concerned since these things will gradually fall in place as we proceed.

For now, purchase only those hooks which we will use in the upcoming tying sessions. They are:

- Size 6 Streamer Hook 4XL
  (or Mustad model 79580)

- Size 10 Nymph Hook 2XL
  (or Mustad model 9671)

- Size 10 Wet Fly Hook
  (or Mustad model 3906)

- Size 12 Dry Fly Hook
  (or Mustad model 94840)

We will go over these hooks carefully during the construction of the flies you will be tying. Incidentally, you will be using these particular hooks for many other patterns for years to come.

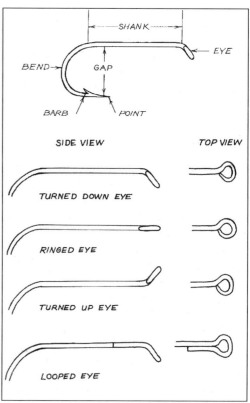

Hook Terminology

## FEATHERS, FURS AND OTHER MATERIALS

In addition to the feathers and furs listed for the patterns you will be tying in the succeeding pages, there are a great variety of materials available to you as a fly tier. Don't worry about them now. Just about every bird and animal has feathers and furs that you can use, and there are ever increasing numbers of artificial or synthetic fabrics and fibers available to us in knitting shops, department stores, and craft-supply houses. All these things will come together step-by-step with each new pattern you learn as you develop your skills.

What you should be aware of now is that there are certain feather and fur items you can obtain without cost. Consider: scraps no longer used by taxidermists; trimmings from fur dealers; by-products from game farms; hides and plumage from friends who hunt; zoos. And last but not least, road hunting, which seems to have become a sport of its own. Many fly tiers will pick up road-killed animals such as squirrels, fox, woodchuck, and others. After skinning, scraping, washing, and drying, eventually the hide (or feathers) can be used for fly tying. If you are interested in saving a few dollars on materials, I suggest you get a copy of the book *Fly Tying Materials* which goes into more depth and detail about road-hunting.

The materials you will be using now will be explained as each pattern is being tied. For now, buy only the materials listed in the succeeding pages.

## ODDS AND ENDS

Anything that will add to your comfort and make life a little easier while you sit at the tying bench should be used. Fly tiers tend to be an inventive lot and over the years I have seen a number of gadgets and improvisations designed to facilitate the construction of one or more intricate patterns. As you go along, I'm sure that most of you will also come up with a few ideas of your own.

Two items that will be of great help are a blotter and a good lamp. For my own tying I place a green desk blotter on my work area. The color green is easy on the eyes and the blotter is soft enough to allow for easier handling of small hooks and other materials. Eventually the blotter will become soiled from use and can be replaced. Every now and then I'll spill a bottle of head cement and the blotter, rather than my desktop, absorbs the mess.

When I was young, I could tie flies by candlelight and I could snip a single feather fiber without wearing glasses. Now I need all the help I can get and that means a good lamp. The best light you can use is the sun. During daylight hours and with the proper exposure near a window (or in mild and windless weather on an outside porch) you tend to see colors as they really are. Standard fluorescent lighting distorts color and for that reason it should not be used in fly tying. An ordinary bulb in a lamp which shines directly on the head of your vise and does not create shadows is best. Currently, I use a lamp with a halogen bulb that transmits light equal to a 150-watt bulb. The angle of the arm and head of the lamp can be adjusted to point just where I want maximum light.

Make yourself comfortable. We're about to begin.

# 2 WOOLLY BUGGER
## An Ideal Beginner's Fly

AS YOU PROGRESS and become more familiar with fly tying, you will find that there are such things as "pattern books"(something like recipe books for cooking) and that each different fly can be identified by its pattern description. All fly-tying books, before going into detail as to how a fly is constructed, should first supply the pattern description, including suggested hooks and threads for the particular fly. Patterns are usually listed in the order of materials as they are tied to the hook shank.

Here then, is the pattern description of the first fly we are going to tie.

| WOOLLY BUGGER (sizes 4-14) | |
|---|---|
| Hook: | Streamer (4XL) |
| Thread: | Black (6/0) |
| Tail: | Black marabou extending a full hook shank length past bend |
| Palmered Rib: | Black saddle hackle palmered (wound in an open spiral) over the body |
| Body: | Dark olive chenille in a size suitable for the hook |

Let's take a closer look at this pattern description and the individual parts before we tie it.

After the name of the fly you will see two numbers in parentheses. These indicate the common hook size range in which this pattern is usually tied — in this case hook sizes 4 through 14. The average pattern size for this fly is normally a 6, 8, or 10. This does not mean you cannot tie it in larger or smaller sizes. This is true for any fly.

## HOOK

The hook listed is slightly shorter than one often used for traditional streamer- or bucktail-type flies. Here we are using a 4XL as opposed to a longer 6XL. This pattern has its basis in the old-time Woolly Worm which has a short tail and is regarded more as a wet fly or nymph than as a streamer. The hook is fairly heavy, has a moderately long shank, and is well suited for this pattern. However this pattern can also be tied on just about any streamer hook from 3XL to 6XL, or for that matter, a salmon fly hook.

## THREAD

This is a suggested type. If you can achieve the same results with another thread, by all means do so. The ideal is always to use as light a thread as possible in order to prevent unnecessary bulk. In a streamer fly, where the thread is used to build up the head, a finer thread, while requiring more wraps, will produce a smoother, neater appearance.

## TAIL

This consists of marabou fibers. This soft, supple, and floppy feather originally came from the marabou stork but the feathers of that bird are now prohibited from importation. Today, the word "marabou," when used in reference to fly tying, refers to the soft, fluffy feather coming from the white domestic turkey. These feathers range in length from one to seven inches. The shorter ones, those just emerging from the skin of the bird, are often called "blood" feathers or "shorts." Both the long and the short feathers are used. When using the long feathers, a section of fibers is cut from the main stem and placed on the hook shank to form a wing or, in this case, a tail. The shorter plumes, up to three inches long, can be used as is since there is almost no center stem.

Marabou is one of the most popular and effective of all materials because it "breathes" when fished. Because the fibers are soft and supple, they compress into a slim, straight baitfish impression when the fly is pulled or darted to imitate a swimming baitfish. During the pause in the retrieve, the fibers open and flare slightly (breathing) not unlike the propulsive action of a squid or the pulsating motion of a jellyfish. This pulsing or breathing action makes the fly appear to be alive. Marabou is also used on jigs and other fishing lures. It can be dyed to any desired color.

## PALMERED RIB

To "palmer a fly" means to wind a hackle through the body of the fly from the bend to a forward position. An "open" palmer is one in which the hackle is wound in a spiral, leaving a space between each winding of hackle. The word "rib" indicates any material which is wound forward in an open spiral to the head or front end of the hook shank.

In our pattern, the Woolly Bugger, a black saddle hackle is to be used as the palmered rib.

An explanation of the word "hackle" is in order since you will be hearing and reading about it throughout your fly-tying career. (If you want to learn more about hackle and its various applications, get a copy of *The Metz Book of Hackle*.) Anytime you see, or hear, the word hackle by itself it always means the feather coming from the neck or back (saddle) of a rooster – a male chicken. A saddle hackle, which we are using in this pattern, comes from the back, or saddle portion, of a rooster. Now and then, you will see reference made to "hen hackle," which refers to the neck or back feathers of the female chicken. Other references, such as partridge hackle, grouse hackle, or even rubber hackle, are preceded by a defining word which identifies them.

What makes rooster hackle unique and extremely useful in fly tying is that most of the fibers that grow from the center stem of the feather are free of the tiny barbules which would, as in other birds, hold the barbs, or individual fibers, together. For example, if you look at a single feather from a duck, goose or turkey wing, you will find that it binds together as one unit. If you take a feather from the neck of a rooster and bend it in an arc, you'll see that the barbs stand out individually. It is this characteristic, inherent in the rooster hackle, that allows us to wind it around a hook shank while the barbs radiate from it freely. Later, when we wind our black saddle hackle as a palmered rib, you'll see this happen for yourself.

## BODY

The pattern calls for an olive chenille suitable for the hook size. Chenille, a yarn manufactured by spinning rayon (or other material) around a thread core, is manufactured in various sizes and colors, is soft to the touch, and is generally used to form the body of a fly – usually a wet fly or streamer fly. In our pattern, it is ribbed with the black saddle hackle. Chenille is one of the most common and least expensive items sold in fly shops. Since this pattern is tied in a fairly wide range of sizes, we want to match the chenille size to the hook being used. Chenille is generally sold wound on cards with sizes designated as follows:

| Size | Description | Diameter | Related Hook Sizes |
|------|-------------|----------|--------------------|
| 00 | Extra Fine | 3/32" | 12 and smaller |
| 0 | Fine | 1/8" | 8-10 |
| 1 | Medium | 5/32" | 4-6 |
| 2 | Large | 3/16" | 1/0-2 |
| 3 | Extra Large | 1/4" | 2/0 and larger |

Now that we've become more familiar with the materials that will be used on our Woolly Bugger, we're ready to tie our first fly. I assure you that this one will be very easy. In fact, you almost can't tie it improperly. The bonus is that this fly may just be one of the most deadly of all streamer-type patterns for taking fish. Here we go.

(Note: The following instructions are for right-handed tiers. For those of you who are southpaws, many of the procedures will take a reverse direction.)

## TO BEGIN

Clamp a size 6 hook in the jaws of your vise. Since this is a fairly large hook (so far as fly tying goes), you may cover the point and barb so that you don't inadvertently cut the thread on the point as you wind your thread. As you become more proficient, however, you should get into the habit of placing the hook in the vise so that only the lower part of the bend is covered. If, on hooks

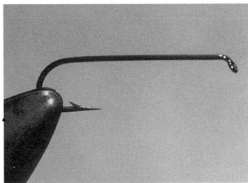

**1** Improper hook placement

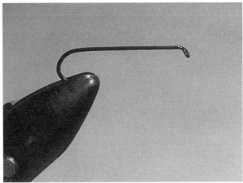

**2** Proper hook placement

**3** Place thread against hook shank

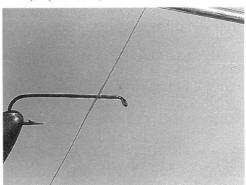

**4** Place fly-line against hook shank

sizes 16 and smaller, you clamp down on the barb area, the weakest part of the hook, you may break it.

Take your bobbin and expose about five inches of thread from the tube. Hold the bobbin in your right hand and the thread between thumb and finger of your left hand. Place the thread against the shank of the hook just behind the hook eye. (To more clearly demonstrate what it is taking place during this process, in photos 4-7 I have substituted a heavy fly line to take the place of the thread. All movements of thread will always be away from you, in a clockwise rotation unless otherwise specified.)

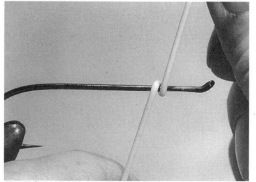

**5** Make turn around shank

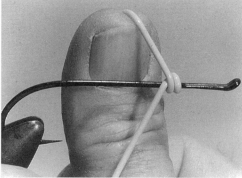

**6** Wind rearward over first wrap

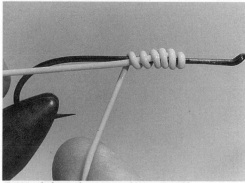

**7** Wind thread rearward over itself

**8** Cut excess thread

**9** Blood marabou and full marabou plume

**10** Select the appropriate marabou

Keeping the thread taut, wind one turn of thread around the hook shank. Pull the thread held between left thumb and forefinger downward so that is it directly under the hook shank and at right angles to it. Take another turn of thread around the shank, but this time pull the thread so it slants to the rear and begins to wind over itself. Continue to wind

the thread around the hook shank in connecting spirals toward the bend. You will be wrapping the thread over itself.

When you have completed five or six turns over that portion of thread held between your left thumb and forefinger, you can cut the loose end next to the hook shank. Or, you can simply keep winding the thread

toward the back of the hook until you reach the bend. Upon reaching it, cut the excess thread.

Take a black marabou plume and cut a section of fibers about an inch and a quarter wide from the center stem; or, if you are using a short or "blood" feather, separate the lower fibers (bottom of stem) from the top fibers and stroke the upper fibers

**11** Cut a section from marabou plume

**12** Measure the upper section

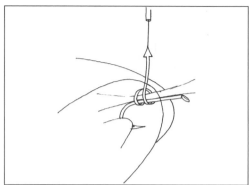

**13** Pass the thread between your fingers

**14** Secure the marabou with thread wraps

**15** Tie down marabou butt ends

**16** Select a black-saddle hackle feather

into a unit or clump.

Place the clump of marabou on top of the hook shank and measure it against the shank so that the tail will be equal in length to the hook shank (from behind the eye to the bend).

Now move the clump to the rear, so that the section that was over the eye is over the bend where you left your thread.

Hold this clump of marabou in place using your left thumb and forefinger while you secure it with thread. With your right hand, grasp the bobbin and bring the thread up against the tip of your left thumb, over the marabou, down against the tip of your left index finger, around the hook shank, and pull the thread taut in an upward direction. (By pulling in an upward direction, you will create a complete loop around the material and hook, thus tightening one to the other concentrically, preventing the material from slipping down the far side of the hook shank.)

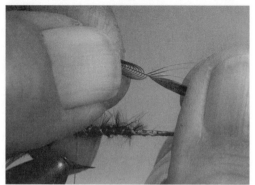

**17** Separate fibers between the tip and butt

**18** Prepared feather ready to tie in

**19** Tie in the saddle-hackle feather

This procedure may feel awkward at first, but you will quickly get used to it. All you are doing is bringing thread around both the marabou clump and the hook shank to tie the marabou in place. It's just that your index finger and thumb are in the way and, therefore, you have to hug the thread against these digits during the process.

You should now be able to remove your left thumb and forefinger and the marabou should stay in place. Just to make sure, however, take a couple more tight turns of thread around the area.

Wind the thread forward covering the loose butt ends of the marabou and then back again to a position before the bend. If the butt ends are long and extend beyond the eye, cut the excess at a point just

behind the eye and spiral the thread over them and the shank, winding to near the eye and again back to the shank. The tail of your fly is now complete.

At this time we are going to tie in a black saddle hackle feather which will later be spiraled, or palmered, forward. The feather needs to be long enough, after having been spiraled around the shank, to reach the eye of the hook. In this case, a length of five inches should do. The fibers growing from the stem should be as long as the width of the hook gap. If they are a little longer, it's okay, but they shouldn't exceed one and a half times the width of the gap.

Take one of these feathers and stroke the fibers near the tip rearward, forcing them from the tip. You

are forming a separation point.

Place the feather against the hook shank, with the tip pointing diagonally downward between the thread and the hook shank. The shiny side of the feather should be against the shank and the dull side should be facing you. (The shiny side of a feather is always darker than the dull side.)

Grasp the bobbin and take two or three turns of thread around the feather stem (where the fibers have been separated from the tip) and the hook shank.

Wind the thread in an open spiral around the shank and the excess tip of the feather, working toward the eye of the hook. When you reach a point an ⅛ inch behind the eye of the hook, cut any excess tip that extends beyond this point. (You are

**20** Wind thread back to bend

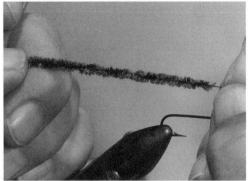

**21** Expose cotton core at end of chenille

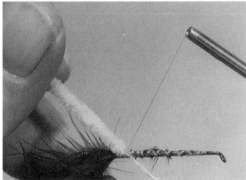

**22** Tie in chenille's cotton core

**23** Wind chenille around the shank

**24** Secure wound chenille with thread wraps

**25** Cut away excess chenille

using the excess tip as part of an underbody to keep the area smooth and free of bumps.) Wind the thread, in an open spiral, rearward to the bend. Leave it there.

Cut a five- or six-inch length of dark-olive chenille. For a size 6 hook a medium size (#1) chenille is just about right. (Chenille used in some photos is white only for purpose of clarity.) Using your thumb and fingernail, strip away a half inch of the chenille fibers from the thread core.

Place the exposed thread core against the hook shank so its end points diagonally downward between the thread and the hook shank.

Take three or four turns of thread around both thread core and hook shank to secure the chenille. Wind the thread forward, in an open spiral, to a position 1/16 of an inch behind the hook eye.

Grasp the chenille and wind it around the hook shank in adjoining spirals (one next to the other) to where the thread hangs.

When you've made your last turn, hold the chenille taut in a vertical position and use your left hand to

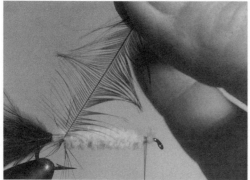

**26** Wind saddle hackle around the chenille body

**27** Wind hackle in open, evenly spaced wraps

**28** Tie off the saddle hackle with thread

**29** Cut away the excess saddle hackle

**30** Woolly Bugger

control the bobbin. Take two turns of thread over and around the chenille and hook shank, thereby securing the chenille to the shank.

Cut away the excess chenille close to the hook. Take two more turns of thread around the chenille and hook shank to make it more secure.

Grasp the black saddle hackle

(tied in earlier) and wind it into and around the chenille body in an open spiral to the thread. Be sure to keep the feather on its back, that is, shiny side against the chenille. If it tends to twist and not want to conform (some hackle stems have irregular shapes and will misbehave), don't worry about it, just keep winding to the head. As you make each turn the

center stem will bite into the chenille causing the feather fibers to stand up and out from the chenille. This is the effect you want.

Upon reaching the thread, hold the hackle feather in an almost vertical position, but leaning slightly beyond the hook eye, and use your left hand to guide the thread from the bobbin as you take two turns of thread around the stem of the feather, securing it to the hook shank.

Snip away the excess hackle feather. Take a few more turns of thread around the head area, covering any exposed hackle or chenille parts that can't be trimmed closely enough with your scissors. Do not try to form a head on this fly. Just finish off with a nice smooth taper.

Make three half-hitch knots with your thread. Instructions for this simple knot (and the more difficult whip finish) follow directly. Using your dubbing needle, place a touch of head cement on the windings.

Take a break – have a cup of coffee, relax. You've earned it.

Now that you've tied your first Woolly Bugger you can, without further instructions, tie all the popular versions of this fly simply by changing the color of the materials. In addition, you have acquired the techniques used in tying the Woolly Worm, the old standby and predecessor of the Woolly Bugger. The following list contains the dressings of the patterns most used. You can also create a few versions of your own, should you be so inclined.

As you can see, the tying of a simple pattern such as the Woolly Bugger has already allowed you to tie a number of other flies in the same style. Each time you tie a new pattern using a slightly different procedure, your general knowledge of techniques expands to include many other patterns.

### BLACK WOOLLY BUGGER

(sizes 4-14)

| | |
|---|---|
| Tail: | Black marabou |
| Rib: | Black saddle hackle, palmered |
| Body: | Black chenille |

### BROWN AND TAN WOOLLY BUGGER

(sizes 4-14)

| | |
|---|---|
| Tail: | Brown marabou |
| Rib: | Brown saddle hackle, palmered |
| Body: | Tan chenille |

### GRIZZLY AND WHITE WOOLLY BUGGER

(sizes 4-14)

| | |
|---|---|
| Tail: | White marabou |
| Rib: | Grizzly saddle hackle. palmered |
| Body: | White chenille |

(Note: All Woolly Buggers use the same hook and thread as described in our original pattern.)

### BLACK WOOLLY WORM

(sizes 4-12)

| | |
|---|---|
| Hook: | 3XL |
| Thread: | Black |
| Tail: | Dyed red hackle fibers |
| Rib: | Fine or medium oval tinsel and grizzly saddle hackle |
| Body: | Black chenille |

You'll see that one difference between the Woolly Worm and the Woolly Bugger is the tail fibers. Here the tail is formed from fibers from a rooster neck feather, which has been dyed red, and they are tied in fairly short. Another difference is that a tinsel ribbing is first wound through the chenille body in an open spiral to the head, and then the grizzly saddle hackle follows, also in an open spiral.

### BROWN WOOLLY WORM

(sizes 4-12)

| | |
|---|---|
| Tail: | Red hackle fibers |
| Rib: | Grizzly hackle, palmered |
| Body: | Brown chenille |

### OLIVE WOOLLY WORM

(sizes 4-12)

| | |
|---|---|
| Tail: | Red hackle fibers |
| Rib: | Grizzly hackle, palmered |
| Body: | Olive chenille |

### YELLOW WOOLLY WORM

(sizes 4-12)

| | |
|---|---|
| Tail: | Red hackle fibers |
| Rib: | Grizzly hackle, palmered |
| Body: | Yellow chenille |

(Note: The only listed pattern which requires a tinsel rib in this series is the Black Woolly Worm. However, you can dress up your flies in this manner if you so desire, and you can construct them in any color you wish. By all means design a Woolly Worm of your own.)

## THE HALF-HITCH KNOT

This is a very simple knot which can be made by manipulating the thread with the fingers of one hand, with a ball-point pen, or with one of the half-hitch tools sold in fly shops.

Let's try it with a ball-point pen. First, make sure the cartridge containing the ink is retracted so that all you have at the working end is a recess or indentation.

**Step 1**. Place the pen against the thread from which the bobbin is hanging.

**Step 2a**. With your left hand holding the bobbin take one turn of thread around the front end of the pen.
**b**. Complete turn of thread around pen.

**Step 3**. Place the open recessed end of the pen over the eye of the hook.

**Step 4**. Slide the thread off the pen and onto the hook shank and pull taut. That's it.

If you use this knot to finish off the head of your fly, you will need three or four half hitches in a row to

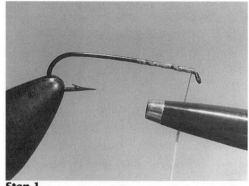
Step 1

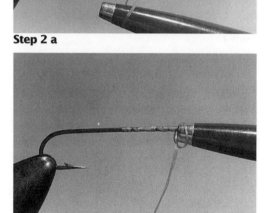
Step 2 a

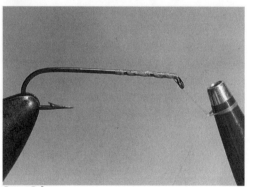
Step 2 b

Step 3 & 4

keep the thread from unravelling, and a touch of head cement for additional security.

A better knot, though a bit more difficult, is the whip-finish knot. There is a tool on the market, the Matarelli whip finisher (the only brand I recommend - it is the same style offered by Orvis) which will make this knot for you. The tool comes with complete instructions. However, I believe it is a good idea for all fly tiers to know the principle of the whip finish, and therefore, it is illustrated here as it should be done, by hand.

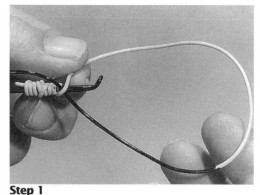

**Step 1**

## THE WHIP-FINISH KNOT

To more clearly illustrate what takes place, I've used a fly line and a very large hook. The fly line, which is one piece, has been painted black so you can see just how it is being tied over itself during the procedure. The black portion of the fly line is the thread that goes to your bobbin and the white line is the portion that is manipulated to make the whip-finish knot.

**Step 1**. Form a loose loop of thread (the white portion of the line) while holding the thread that goes to your bobbin (the black portion of the line) against the hook shank at an angle.

**Step 2.** Catch this (black) thread against the shank by bringing the loop (white) up and over it, and then

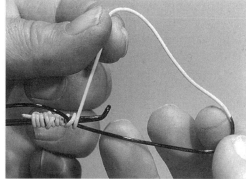

**Step 2**

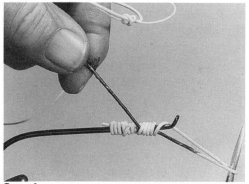

**Step 4**

wrapping the loop around the hook shank.

**Step 3**. Continue wrapping the loop (white) around the thread going to your bobbin (black) and the hook shank for three additional turns.

**Step 4.** When you have completed four wraps (white) around the thread

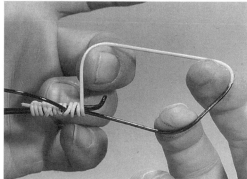

**Step 3**

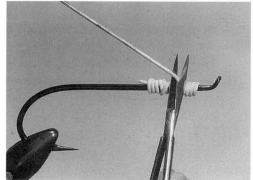

**Step 5**

going to your bobbin (black) and the hook shank, slip a dubbing needle into the loop to hold it under tension. Next, pull on the thread going to the bobbin (black) to close the loop. Slip the needle from the loop as the knot snugs down.

**Step 5.** Clip the tag end of the thread and the whip finish is complete.

# 3 DARK HENDRICKSON NYMPH
## A Foundation in Nymph Tying

THE NEXT FLY is an excellent example that shows the techniques used in the construction of many nymph patterns. It is not difficult to tie, and, when fished, it simulates many forms of subsurface insect life. The name of this pattern is the Dark Hendrickson Nymph. Let's take a closer look at the components.

**DARK HENDRICKSON NYMPH**
(sizes 10-14)

| | |
|---|---|
| Hook: | 2XL, regular or heavy wire |
| Thread: | Gray |
| Tail: | Wood-duck or partridge hackle fibers |
| Rib: | Fine oval tinsel or gold wire |
| Abdomen: | Muskrat dubbing fur (or other natural gray fur) |
| Wing case: | Mallard duck wing-quill section (or equivalent) |
| Legs: | Wood-duck or partridge hackle fibers (or equivalent) |
| Thorax: | Muskrat dubbing fur (or equivalent) more heavily applied than abdomen |

Before we clamp a hook in the vise, let's review the materials needed for this pattern.

The hook is a standard type for nymphs; it is made of fairly heavy steel (so it will sink more rapidly) and is longer than a normal shank length (2XL). The extra length is specified because the natural insect in its nymphal stage has a longish shape.

We're using gray thread because it complements the overall color of the body.

The tail of the pattern calls for wood-duck flank fibers. These feathers, which are lemon-brown in color with fine black barring running through them, come from the male American wood duck. Though they are not scarce, they are hard to come by and fairly expensive. If you have friends who hunt ducks, ask them to save these (and other feathers) for you.

For beginners, I recommend the use of mallard flank fibers instead of natural wood duck for the sole reason that you will be educating your fingers with a less costly material. Flank feathers from the male mallard duck are more plentiful and are easily dyed to imitate the natural wood-duck color. They are sold as "wood-duck substitute" in most fly shops. You can, if you have a supply of mallard flank on hand and are ambitious, dye your own. Some mail-order houses sell a specially formulated dye just so fly tiers can obtain a wood-duck shade. It can also be obtained by using one of the common household dyes such as Rit or Tintex. In this case, you will have to mix yellow with a touch of brown to duplicate the color.

Some fly tiers like to use partridge hackle for the tail of this pattern, and that's fine since it also imitates the natural insect. However, partridge may be more difficult to obtain than natural wood duck. In this case, I'm referring to the neck and body feathers of the Hungarian partridge. These range in color from speckled brown to speckled gray.

You can use other feathers which have a similar barring for the tail or legs. Many game birds, and the backs or saddles of hen chickens, have the desired markings. As long as you imitate the natural mottling, or color break-up, inherent in the tails or legs of the natural insect, you can use it.

**Rib**: I've given a choice between fine oval tinsel and gold wire. Generally, I will use the oval tinsel on larger flies such as those tied on a size 10 or 12 hook, and I use gold wire on hook sizes 14 and smaller. The purpose of the gold rib is to create a glitter or sparkle emanating from the body, and it also gives the impression of segmentation found in the abdomen of the natural insect.

**Abdomen (or body)**: Here, we are using the underfur from a muskrat or other animal with gray fur. If you wish to use one of the synthetic furs or blends in gray, that's acceptable, because this is an underwater pattern and synthetic furs usually sink rapidly.

You will find that nearly all animal hides are comprised of both long, and sometimes stiff, fibers called guard hairs and shorter, softer fibers called underfur. If you are cutting the fur from a piece of skin, hold the guard hairs and, after having cut the clump from the skin, comb the underfur from it. (I use a fine-tooth comb for this.) Guard hairs, which are mixed in with the underfur, create problems because they protrude from what should be a neatly tapered body. (There are times, as you'll see later, when furs with guard hairs mixed in serve a special purpose.)

**Wing Case**: The immature nymph has a protective skin under which the adult's wings grow. As they gradually enlarge, the wings create a prominent bump above the thorax which we call the wing case. To imitate this wing case, we are going to use one of the flight feathers from a mallard duck, or other similar waterfowl. These feathers are slate gray in color and are sold in virtually all fly shops. It is less expensive to buy a matched (a left and a right) pair of wings, which contain eight usable flight feathers on each wing, as opposed to buying individual pairs. Again, if you have any friends who hunt, ask them to save the wings for you. Other ducks with wing quills that can be used are widgeon, pintail, canvasback or any of the larger species.

**Legs**: Here we use the same material we used for the tail.

**Thorax**: This is an extension of the abdomen. Abdomen and thorax together form the body of the fly. The same material is used for both.

Now that we've become familiar with the materials used in the Dark

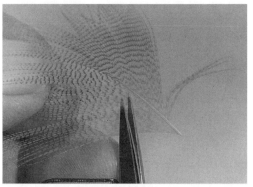

**1** Cut fibers from the wood-duck flank feather

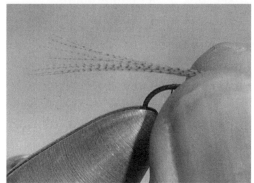

**2** Measure fibers for tail length

Hendrickson Nymph, let's tie one.

Affix a size 10 hook in your vise. This time, try leaving the point and barb exposed. Spiral gray thread onto the hook shank beginning behind the eye and wind it to the bend.

Take a wood-duck feather (or dyed mallard substitute) and cut a

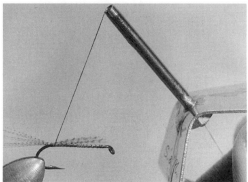

**3** Tie fibers in to form tail

**4** Tie oval tinsel to the shank

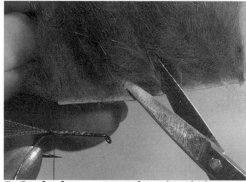

**5** Cut fur from a piece of muskrat hide

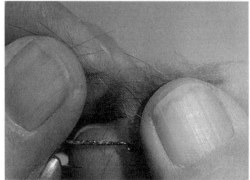

**6** Remove guard hairs from the muskrat fur

section containing six to seven fibers from the feather. The cut should be made near, or next to, the center stem of the feather.

Keep the tips aligned and transfer the section (as a complete unit or clump) to the thumb and forefinger of your right hand. Measure it against the hook so that the tips

extend a distance of two hook-gape widths past the bend. In other words, the tail should be twice as long as the hook gape is wide.

While keeping the clump in place over the hook shank, transfer it to the thumb and forefinger of your left hand. Secure the tail fibers to the hook shank with a couple turns of thread. (This is the same procedure as when you tied in the marabou tail on the Woolly Bugger. If you've forgotten, go back and check out the detailed maneuver.) Wind the thread forward over the exposed portion of butt fibers and then back to the bend once more.

Tie in one end of a four- to five-inch section of fine oval gold tinsel at the bend and forget about it for now.

Now we are going to "dub" with fur. To "dub" simply means to spin fur (natural or synthetic) onto thread, so a tapered fur body will be formed when the thread is wound around the shank. When fly tiers refer to "dubbing," they are talking about a particular kind of fur or fur blend.

The simplest method of spinning fur onto thread is by placing it against a waxed section of thread and twisting it with thumb and forefinger. Cut a section of fur from the base of a piece of muskrat hide (if you're using a pre-blended and pre-packaged wad of fur that is sold in fly shops you won't have to bother with this procedure). Remove all the guard hairs.

Take the underfur (which now has had all the guard hairs removed)

**7** Wax the thread

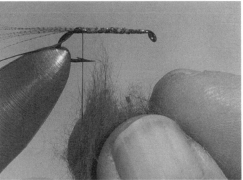

**8** Touch the dubbing to the waxed thread

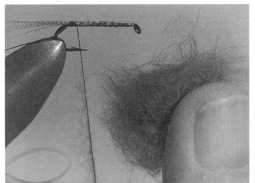

**9** The dubbing fur adheres to the thread

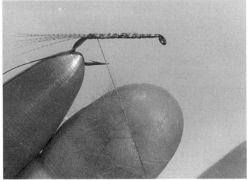

**10** Place index finger against dubbed thread

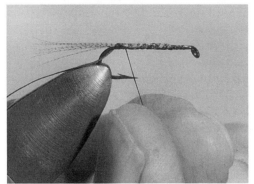

**11** Slide your thumb across your index finger

and pull the fibers apart, and then shove them together again. Repeat this five or six times. The idea is to get the fibers to intermingle or blend into one another so they are not stringy. They "dub" better when they are meshed and mixed up. You can obtain quicker and better results if you mix them in a blender. In this case, it's a good idea to purchase a

blender of your own since wives and mothers frown upon finding hair or fur in their own processors.

Expose about two or three inches of thread between the bobbin tip and the hook shank. Even though you may be using a pre-waxed thread, add a little more wax until your fingers get used to spinning and twisting fur onto thread. If you use one of

the sticky waxes that comes in a push-up stick container, you only have to touch the dubbing wad against the thread to make it adhere.

Pick a very small amount of fur from the blended ball of fur you've made and place it against the thread. Try to shape it a bit so that it stretches along the thread and is not all clumped in one area. It can be pushed up and down and positioned.

Close your left thumb and forefinger on the now-furry thread and roll your finger off your thumb. This is the same motion you would use if you were to snap your fingers, but do it slower with less pressure. Don't be afraid to use pressure. Do not roll your thumb and forefinger back and forth. Always keep them going in one direction in repeated snap-type motions, but without actually climax-

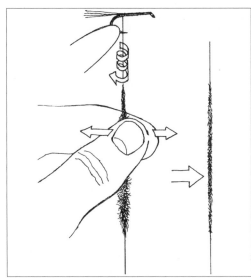

Always roll your thread in the same direction when you apply dubbing. Spinning the thread back and forth will not apply dubbing tightly and will cause your fly's body to be loose, shaggy, and not at all durable.

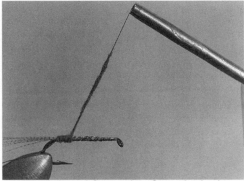

**12** Wind thread forward to form the body

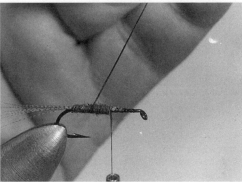

**13** Wind oval tinsel forward to form the rib; cut away the excess oval tinsel

ing in a snap. The fur should now be clinging tightly to the thread. Try to make that portion closest to the hook shank as thin as possible, tapering to a slightly heavier diameter near the bobbin tip. You're now ready to form the body of your fly.

Wind the dubbed thread around the hook shank in tight and barely overlapping spirals to a point on the hook shank just slightly past center. Try to form an ever increasing taper

as you wind the dubbed thread forward. If you've used too much fur, remove it and start over. If you've not used enough, just spin some more onto the thread. After a while you'll get so good at this you'll pluck the exact amount every time. Leave the thread where it is.

Grasp the oval tinsel and wind it forward around the body in an open spiral to the thread. Tie it down with the thread and secure it well. Cut away the excess tinsel. We're about halfway there. You've earned a five-minute breather.

Now it's time to tie in the duck-wing quill section which will later form the wingcase. Cut an ⅛-inch section of fibers from the center stem of a mallard wing-quill feather (or other large, gray duck quill). Cut

an ⅛-inch section of fibers from the center stem.

With the underside (on duck quills this is the shiny side) facing upward and the tip pointing toward or beyond the eye of the hook, place the quill section on top of the hook shank (hold it there with left thumb and forefinger) and tie it down with four or five turns of thread. Clip away any excess directly in back of the eye. Forget about this feather for now.

Spin more fur onto your thread and fill in that area between where the wing-quill feather was just tied down and the hook eye. There should be more fur in this, the thorax area, than on the abdomen (to match the thicker thorax of the natural insect). As you make your turns

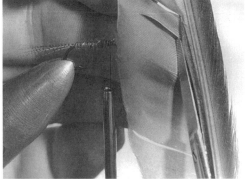

**14** Cut fibers from a mallard wing quill

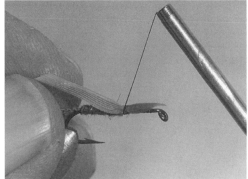

**15** Tie the quill section to the hook shank

**16** Wind dubbed thread to form the thorax

**17** Complete the dubbed thorax area

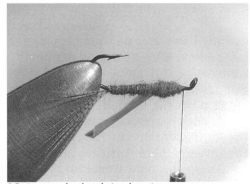

**18** Invert the hook in the vise

**19** Measure wood duck fibers for length

of dubbed thread, place a couple of them against the wing-case feather so that when it is later folded forward it will form a slight hump. (You can place one or two turns directly against the edge of the feather where it emerges from under the thread.)

When you've achieved a nice full thorax, leave the thread hanging from its bobbin just behind the eye of the hook. (Don't get too close to the eye.)

Remove the unfinished fly from the vise and reclamp it in the jaws in an upside-down position.

Cut a section of eight or nine wood-duck fibers (or partridge) from a feather, keeping the tips aligned.

Measure them so that when they are tied in the tips of the fibers will just reach the point of the hook.

These will resemble the legs of the living nymph. Hold them in place with your left thumb and forefinger and tie them down securely with thread. Take one turn of thread between the fibers and the hook shank so that the fibers point slightly upward and directly at and to the hook point. Clip excess.

Leave the thread dangling by the

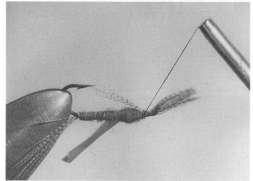

**20** Tie the wood duck fibers to the shank

**21** Return the hook to the upright position

**22** Pull the quill forward beyond the hook eye

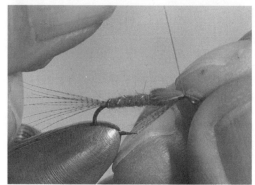

**23** Tie the mallard quill down with thread

**24** Apply cement to the head

**25** Dark Hendrickson Nymph

weight of the bobbin just behind the hook eye.

Remove the fly from the vise and re-insert it once more in an upright position, the way it was before.

Grasp the duck-quill section tied in previously and pull it forward, straight out over the hook eye. The section should cup and surround the top portion of dubbed fur.

Hold the duck-quill section taut with your right thumb and forefinger (extending beyond the hook eye). Use your left hand to take three or four turns of thread around the quill section just behind the hook eye.

Once it has been secured, clip the excess butt-section fibers. Take enough turns of thread around any exposed ends to form a neatly

tapered head. Half hitch or whip finish with the thread and cut it away.

With your dubbing needle, place a drop of head cement on the thread windings and give the wing case a coat of cement. This gives the wing case a shiny appearance in addition to making it more durable.

Your first nymph deserves a celebration.

# 4 GOLD-RIBBED HARE'S EAR NYMPH
## An All-Purpose Subsurface Fly

THE NEXT PATTERN we are going to tie may be one of the most popular nymphs in the country. It's called the Gold-ribbed Hare's Ear nymph and, except for a tail of brown hackle fibers and a wingcase exactly like the one you've just learned, the entire fly is made from the hairs and fur of an English rabbit mask (face) and ears. This pattern teaches another dubbing technique that you will be able to use whenever coarse furs or fibers are required for the body. Let's take a closer look at the description.

### GOLD-RIBBED HARE'S EAR NYMPH
(sizes 8-16)

| | |
|---|---|
| Hook: | 1X or 2X long |
| Thread: | Brown or tan |
| Tail: | Brown hackle fibers (half a shank length past bend) |
| Underbody: | Fine lead wire |
| Rib: | Fine oval gold tinsel |
| Abdomen: | Hare's-mask dubbing |
| Wing case: | Mottled-turkey wing quill or duck wing quill |
| Thorax: | Hare's mask and ears dubbing |
| Legs: | Picked out guard hairs and fibers from thorax |

The primary component of this fly, dubbing from the hare's mask and ears, can be found in all fly shops. You will even see some dealers offering masks and dubbing in dyed colors. This particular fur comes from the English hare, imported from England and other parts of Europe. A good substitute is the fur and guard hairs of the Eastern pine squirrel. Our native rabbit's fur does not seem to have the coarseness or texture of the English hare.

The wing case on this pattern is usually constructed from the inner flight feathers of a brown or wild turkey. These feathers are mottled brown and white and vary from light to dark tones. It is this break-up of color which adds a buggy look to the imitation. Mottled-turkey wing quills, which are also used in the Muddler Minnow and nearly all hopper patterns, are rather scarce today (farmers raise only white birds for consumption), and they are quite expensive. These feathers exist on the wild turkey which is hunted in most states. If you hunt, or have friends who hunt, ask them to save these feathers for you. Let's tie the fly.

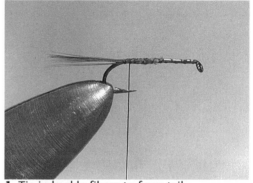

1 Tie in hackle fibers to form tail

Affix a size 10, 2XL nymph hook in your vise. Spiral the thread onto the hook shank, beginning behind the eye and winding to the rear to a place on the shank that is just over the hook point.

Pull a section of six or seven fibers from a natural brown rooster neck feather, and tie them in with the tips extending half a shank length past the bend. (Use the same technique employed when tying in the wood-duck flank on the previous fly.) Make sure to cover the butts with the thread and then bring the thread back to its starting position at the bend.

Cut a four-inch length of fine oval

**2** Tie fine oval tinsel to shank

**3** Wrap lead wire around the hook shank

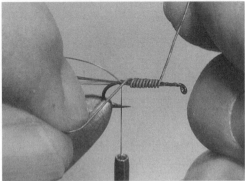

**4** Finish wrapping lead wire on the hook shank

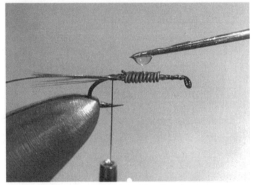

**5** Apply head cement to the lead wire

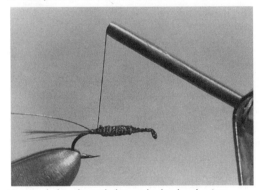

**6** Wind the thread through the lead wire

gold tinsel and tie in one end at the bend. Clip any excess and leave the thread at a position on the shank that's halfway between the hook barb and the hook point

Because this fly is intended to be fished deep, it requires an underbody of lead wire.

Cut a six-inch section of fine

(.016 diameter) lead wire, and, while holding one end, simply wrap the wire around the shank in adjoining coils starting from where the thread is hanging and ending at a point ¼ of an inch behind the eye of the hook. Cut the excess wire at both ends. Apply a coat of head cement to the wrapped coils of lead wire.

Wind the thread through the lead wire. Wind a few extra turns against the front end of the wire to build up a slight taper. Wind back through the coils again, and wind a few turns of thread up against the rear end of the lead wire, also tapering that end. The use of head cement and thread is to keep the wire from rotating around the shank. Now wind the thread back to the tail.

Our next step is to prepare the dubbing. If you purchased a hare's mask with ears attached, you'll notice that the fur on the face portion is softer than that of the ears. In fact, the fuzz growing on the ears is not soft at all, but fairly coarse and prickly, and usually much darker.

With your scissors cut two small piles of hair; one pile coming from

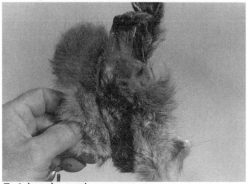

**7** A hare's mask

**8** Cut fur from the hare's mask

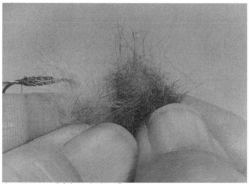

**9** Mix and blend the fur

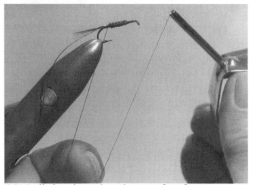

**10** Pull the thread with your forefinger

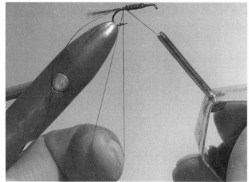

**11** Tie thread down and complete the loop

the softer tan portion of the face and the other from the darker, coarser part. Do not remove any of the guard hairs. If they are unduly long, cut them in half, but in general, leave the prickly fibers alone. Mix the two piles by intermingling them with your fingers (mush them together and pull them apart a few times), or place the two piles in a coffee grinder and blend them. When they are fairly well blended, make a thin rectangular wad about an inch and a half long and half an inch wide. You'll have to tease and stroke the pile of fur apart to accomplish this. If it doesn't come out exactly right, don't worry, it will work well anyway. Place this long wad of dubbing on the table within easy reach.

Pull six inches of thread from your bobbin. Place your left forefinger against the center of the thread. (Between the bobbin tip and where the thread is attached to the hook shank.)

While pressing your left forefinger against the center of the exposed thread, bring the bobbin tip up to the hook shank at the bend, thus forming a loop.

With the bobbin wind four or five turns of thread around the shank at the bend area, working to the rear so the thread wraps over itself and is secured. Then spiral the thread forward to a position just past the center of the hook shank. Let the bobbin dangle there.

12 Coat one side of the loop with cement

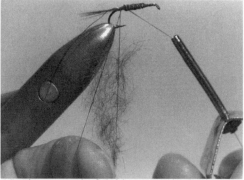

13 Place a wad of dubbing inside the loop

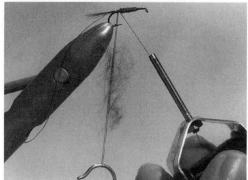

14 Place crook of dubbing needle inside the loop

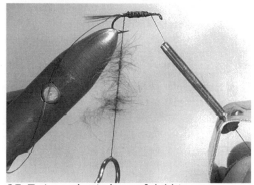

15 Twist and spin loop of dubbing

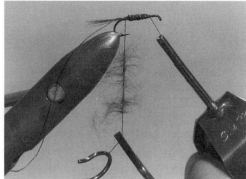

16 Grasp rope with hackle pliers

Pick up your dubbing needle and paint both strands of the loop of thread with head cement (or nail polish).

Place the rectangular wad of dubbing inside the thread loop. Insert the crook of the dubbing needle into the loop, remove your finger, and allow the loop to close. If you don't

have a Matarelli-type dubbing needle, use a crochet hook or paper clip for this procedure. The fur should now be trapped in the thread loop. Now you can adjust and reposition the fur more evenly up and down the length of the thread loop.

Spin the dubbing needle to the left (counterclockwise from below)

until the fur and thread become like a twisted rope or furry noodle.

Clamp the hackle pliers on the furry rope just above the crook of the dubbing needle. Remove the dubbing needle from the loop while keeping light tension on the thread with the hackle pliers.

Wind the fur rope forward around the hook shank in tightly adjoining turns up to the thread position. As you wind forward, try to establish a progressive taper. To accomplish this you may have to slightly overlap the dubbing wraps. When you reach the tying thread, tie the fur rope down securely and clip away the excess.

If the body looks overly scraggly, don't be disappointed. Bodies made this way sometimes have unusual

**17** Wind fur rope around shank

**18** Tie down the furry rope

**19** Trim the excess

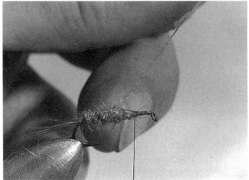
**20** Spiral oval tinsel through the body

**21** Tie in the turkey wing quill

lumps. Just use your scissors to trim those unnatural clumps and wisps. When you're done, the body should still look scraggly but tapered. The fact is, it's almost impossible to tie this fly so badly that it won't take fish. The fuzzier the fly is, the better it works.

Grasp the oval tinsel (tied in earlier) and wind it forward in an open spiral to the thread and tie it down. Clip the excess.

Cut a ⅛-inch-wide section of fibers from a mottled-turkey wing quill, or, if you don't have this feather, use the section from a brown or gray duck or goose quill. Tie it on top of the hook shank exactly as you did when preparing the wing case of the previous fly, the Dark Hendrickson Nymph. Forget about it for now. Bring the thread forward to the eye.

For the thorax, which will be even buggier in appearance than the abdomen, cut some of the short, prickly fibers from the ears of the hare and work them into some of the fur you have left over from before. We want the thorax to be extra prickly.

Form a loop of thread as you did for the abdomen, cement both sides of the loop and add another wad of elongated fur to form another fur rope. Wind this fur rope in tightly adjoining turns to the eye. You may have to resort to exaggerated over-

**22** Wind fur rope forward to form thorax

**23** Pull the quill forward and tie it down

**24** Apply head cement to the wing case and head

**25** Use a dubbing needle to pick fibers for legs

**26** Gold-ribbed Hare's Ear Nymph

lapping, and you might possibly have to repeat the process since the thorax should be fuller and more heavily padded than the abdomen.

When the thorax has been completed, leave the thread at a position just behind the eye. Now, grasp the wingcase feather (whether turkey, duck, or goose) and pull it forward beyond the hook eye. While holding it taut with your right thumb and forefinger, secure it to the shank with thread using your left hand.

Trim away the excess butts from the wing-case feather; wind your thread around any exposed butts while forming a neatly tapered head; whip finish or half hitch and add a drop of head cement to both the windings and the top of the wing-case feather. Remove the fly from the vise. We're almost done.

Take your dubbing needle and pick out bits of fur from beneath the thorax to simulate legs. Make these hairy fibers protrude and hang down from under the thorax so they will be free to pulse and vibrate in the water and entice the fish.

Now, we're done. By the way, do fish this fly. No matter how ugly you think it looks, it really does take fish.

Now that you can tie a couple of basic nymphs, you can apply the techniques to a number of others. The following are just a few of the patterns you will be able to construct after having read the recipes.

**BLUE WING OLIVE NYMPH**
(sizes 14-18)
Hook:       1XL nymph
Thread:     Olive
Tail:       Wood-duck flank fibers
Rib:        Brown cotton thread or single strand brown floss
Body:       Gray/brown/olive dubbing (a blend of these three colors)
Wing case:  Dark gray goose quill section
Legs:       Brown partridge or equivalent (tied as in Dark Hendrickson Nymph)

**MUSKRAT NYMPH**
(sizes 10-16)
Hook:       1XL nymph
Thread:     Black
Tail:       None
Body:       Muskrat dubbing
Legs:       Natural guinea hen fibers (tied in as you would partridge hackle)
Head:       Black ostrich herl (This is tied in behind the eye. Two turns of ostrich forms the fuzzy head.)

**LIGHT CAHILL NYMPH**
(sizes 10-16)
Hook:       2XL Nymph
Thread:     Yellow
Tail:       Wood-duck flank fibers
Body:       Creamy yellow dubbing
Wing case:  Mallard flank feather section
Legs:       Dark cream hackle (tied in as you would partridge legs)

**BEAVER NYMPH**
(sizes 10-16)
Hook:       2XL nymph
Thread:     Gray
Tail:       Wood-duck flank fibers
Rib:        Fine gold wire
Body:       (Abdomen and thorax) Medium-gray beaver dubbing
Legs:       Brown partridge or equivalent (tied as in Dark Hendrickson nymph)

As I said, this is just a partial list of all the nymphs you can tie now. If you check some of the fly-pattern books available, you will be able to find a number of others within the scope of your ever increasing expertise.

# 5 LEADWING COACHMAN
## A Classic Wet Fly

IT'S ODD THAT the wet fly no longer enjoys the popularity it did forty or fifty years ago. Yet it is the fly style that seems to produce fish when all else fails. Sometimes we become too enamored of new fashions and designs in fly dressing and tend to ignore the flies that have proven so successful in the past. The wet fly, the easiest to fish and among the simplest to tie, should be in every trout fisherman's fly box. After all, trout can't read and they still survive by instincts developed over thousands of years. In short, the wet fly looks like something good to eat and trout like that.

Most wet flies use standard methods and techniques in their construction. If you can tie one or two patterns, you can tie most of the others. For our lesson we're going to tie one that is, perhaps, among the top three in effectiveness and popularity. It serves not only to imitate a drowned mayfly, but more important, it represents an emerging or ovipositing caddis. It's the Leadwing Coachman—here is its description and its components. Even the pattern description itself seems simple, doesn't it ?

**LEADWING COACHMAN**
(sizes 10-16)

| | |
|---|---|
| Hook: | Standard wet fly or 1XL wet fly |
| Thread: | Black |
| Tail: | None |
| Body: | Peacock herl |
| Hackle: | Brown (hen preferred) |
| Wing: | Mallard duck wing quill sections |

Let's take a closer look at the ingredients.

The hook, of standard length, is commonly used for wet flies. However, I've listed the option of a 1XL (extra long) model which is just a bit longer in the shank. If you feel there is not enough room on the standard shank, by all means use the longer alternative.

This fly has no tail, though most wet flies do. This pattern is more representative of emerging and ovipositing caddisflies, which, unlike mayflies and stoneflies, have no tails

The body consists of two strands of peacock herl which are taken from the eyed tail feather of a peacock, or male peafowl. It is this long tail feather that the male bird flares and

1 An eyed peacock tail

fans in splendor, especially during courtship. This item is to a fly shop what a loaf of bread is to a supermarket. It is one of the most frequently used materials in fly tying.

When you purchase an eyed peacock tail feather, check to make sure it has a very full eye and that the herled fibers just below the eye have long and heavy flues (barbules).

The finer flues found on herls from the middle and lower part of the tail feather should only be used for winging streamer flies. Don't buy or use what is sold as "strung peacock herl" for this pattern or any wet or dry fly that calls for a body made of peacock herl. Strung herl is usually too skimpy for this purpose.

2 Cut two herls from below the eye

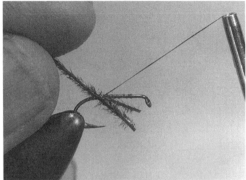

3 Tie two herls to the hook shank

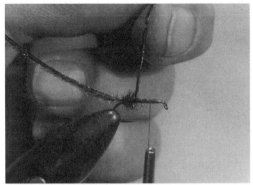

4 Wind one herl forward to the thread

5 Tie down the first herl

6 Wind thread to the bend

7 Wind the second herl forward

Affix a size 10 hook in your vise and wrap the thread onto the shank in an open spiral from the eye to the bend.

From an eyed peacock tail feather, cut two herled fibers from the stem at a point two inches below the eye.

Place the two fibers against the hook shank so that the butt ends almost reach the eye. Wind your thread in close spirals around the butt ends of the herl and the hook shank, wrapping from the bend to a point behind the hook eye.

Wind one of the herls around the shank in tight side-by-side spirals, forward to the thread, and tie it down securely. (Three turns of thread should do it.) Now wind your thread back to the bend in an open spiral, then return it to the starting point behind the hook eye. You are crisscrossing the herl, reinforcing it with wraps of thread.

Grasp the second peacock herl and wind it in side-by-side spirals

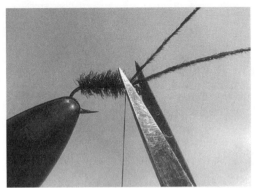

**8** Cut away the excess butts

**9** Isolate the tip of a brown hen feather

**10** Tie the hackle feather to the shank

(over the first herl) to the thread and tie it down. Cut away the excess ends.

Peacock herl is fairly fragile and easily cut by a trout's teeth, so by reinforcing the first herl with the thread, should the outer layer of herl be cut by a fish, you need only remove it and you will have a second body of herl to work with. Don't crisscross the second herl because we want the fibers to be free and to be able to pulse when fished. So far, pretty easy. Right?

We're now ready to tie in the hackle to represent the legs of the natural insect.

Normally, when a pattern description reads: "Hackle: Brown" it means that a feather from a natural brown rooster neck should be used to form a hackle collar. When tying wet flies, tiers often prefer to use wet-fly hackle, i.e. hackle that is soft and webby. In this age of genetically raised roosters, most of the hackle is fairly stiff (making it excellent for dry flies) but it is difficult to find really soft rooster hackle. So, most tiers have switched to using hen hackle to form beards or collars to represent the legs of these subsurface patterns. If you can obtain a brown hen neck, or a saddle having the appropriate-size fibers on its feathers, by all means do so. If all you have is a brown rooster neck, use a feather from that. The technique for both feathers is the same.

You need a feather, the fiber lengths of which, when tied in, just reach the point of the hook. For now, take an educated guess at this, then on succeeding flies you will be better able to judge the proper proportion.

Take a brown feather and separate the fibers from the tip the way you did with the first fly (Woolly Bugger) described in chapter 1.

Hold the feathers against the hook shank so the tip end points diagonally downward between the thread and the hook eye. The shiny side of the feather should be facing you.

Secure the feather to the hook shank by taking five or six turns around the stem of the feather where the fibers have been separated from the tip portion. Clip away the excess tip. Take a couple more turns of thread around the area to make sure the feather is well secured and won't

**11** The hackle feather secured to the shank

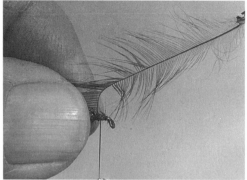

**12** Stroke the fibers to the rear

**13** Fibers "trained" to lie rearward

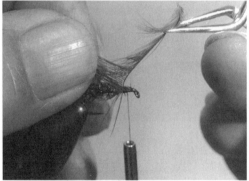

**14** Wind in the hackle feather

**15** Tie off the completed collar

pull out when you wind it. Leave the thread 1⁄32 inch behind the eye. This will give you about a 1⁄16 inch of space to work in. Lift the feather to a vertical position. The shiny side of the feather should now face the hook eye. This is important. If the shiny side does not face the hook eye, unwind the thread and remove the feather and begin again, manipulating it so the shiny side faces to the right, or toward the eye of the hook.

Hold the feather taut with your right hand, but not so tight that you pull it from under the thread windings. With your left thumb and forefinger, stroke the fibers to the rear, toward the bend. A little moisture on the pad of the left thumb and finger helps in this technique. You'll see that the fibers gradually begin to slant back. You only need about a one-inch section of fibers that are slanting to the rear.

After the fibers have been programmed or "folded," attach your hackle pliers to the stem of the feather and begin to wind the feather around the shank.

Each turn around the shank should be in front of the other, in connecting turns, working toward the eye. Three turns around the shank should be enough.

Once you have made three turns of the feather around the hook shank, hold the feather almost vertically erect but slanting slightly toward the eye, and bind it down

16 Trim the fibers from the top of the shank

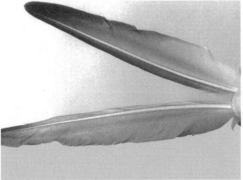
17 A pair of mallard wing quills

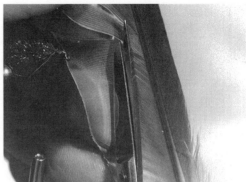
18 Cut fibers from a wing quill

19 Hold far-side quill section with finger

with the thread. Three more turns of thread should secure it. Cut away the excess feather.

With your scissors, cut away those hackle fibers on top of the hook shank only. This insures a better foundation for the wing.

You have secured the hackle fibers in such a manner that none of

the fibers has been bound down with thread, so they are able to move and pulse freely when fished. You will use this technique, called folding the hackle, in many future patterns.

All that remains is to wing the fly.

Many wet flies use a matched pair of sections (left and right) from the wing quills of ducks such as mallards, widgeons, canvasbacks, and others. The very best feathers from these relatively large ducks are the third and fourth on the wing (counting in from the outer flight feather). These have more width and a gentler curve. When we use these quill sections, the thread should only come down on the outer portion of the feather, not the glossy and harder inside. Note that there is a line of

demarcation running down along the inside of each of these feathers; the outer side looks dull while the inner portion nearer the center stem is glossy.

Cut an ⅛-inch section of fibers (as a unit) from a left wing quill feather and another ⅛-inch section from a right wing quill feather. When these sections are tied onto the hook, they should curve toward each other.

Using tweezers, pick up the section that will form the far side of the wing. Measure it against the hook shank so the tip flares upward in a direction that's opposite to the hook bend. It should almost mirror the bend. Place the lower edge on top and just slightly to the side of the fly body. (It should not be placed directly on top, nor should it be allowed to

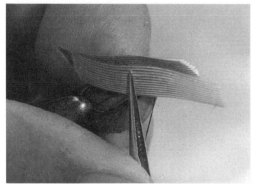

**20** Put near-side quill section in place

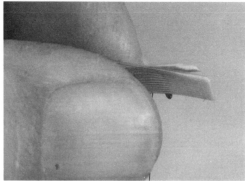

**21** Hold both sections between your fingers

**22** Tie and secure both quills to shank

**23** Cut away the excess butts

**24** Leadwing Coachman

slip down on the side of the hook.) Hold it in position with your left forefinger.

With your tweezers pick up the other section of duck quill and measure it against the one you are holding in place. When it is perfectly aligned with the other, place your left thumb over it and pinch both

wing quills against your left forefinger. Keep both sections in place.

Remove the tweezers. (Simply slide them out from between your left thumb and forefinger.)

Bring the thread up against the thumb pad of your left hand, over the quill sections, downward against your finger pad, under the hook

shank and then up again. Pull the thread tight. Repeat the procedure so both sections are secured. (This is the same technique you learned when you tied in the tail of your first fly, the Woolly Bugger. Here we are using it to secure wings.)

The wings are now in place. Add two more turns of thread to secure them. Clip away the excess butts and then wind enough turns of thread to cover any exposed ends. Do not build up the thread; the smaller the head, the easier it is to affix a leader tippet for fishing.

Half hitch or whip finish your thread and cut it. Place a drop of head cement on the windings.

Your first wet fly, the Leadwing Coachman, is completed.

The techniques used in this pattern, combined with what you've learned previously, allow you to tie the following wet-fly patterns without additional instructions.

## BLACK GNAT
(sizes 8-16)

Hook: Wet fly
Thread: Black
Tail: None
Body: Fine black chenille
(or black dubbing)
Hackle: Black
Wing: Mallard wing quill sections.

## BLUE DUN
(sizes 10-16)

Hook: Wet fly
Thread: Black
Tail: Medium-gray hackle fibers
Body: Muskrat dubbing
Hackle: Medium gray
Wing: Mallard duck quill section

## GOLD-RIBBED HARE'S EAR
(sizes 8-16)

Hook: Wet fly, 1XL
Thread: Black
Tail: Brown hackle fibers
Rib: Fine oval gold tinsel
Body: A blend of hare's mask and
ear dubbing
Wing: Mallard duck quill sections
Hackle: Plucked out guard hairs
from thorax area

You tied this pattern as a nymph. The only difference here is that as a wet fly, it has the mallard wings instead of a wing case.

## BLUE-WING OLIVE
(sizes 14-18)

Hook: Wet fly
Tail: Dark-dun hackle fibers
Body: Medium olive with a hint of
gray dubbing
Hackle: Dark dun
Wing: Mallard wing quill section

## ROYAL COACHMAN
(sizes 10-16)

Hook: Wet fly, 1XL
Thread: Black
Tail: Golden pheasant tippets
Body: Peacock herl divided by a
narrow band of red floss
Hackle: Brown
Wing: White duck wing quill sections

After a couple of turns of peacock to begin the body, a strand of red floss is tied in and wound two or three turns around the center of the shank. The excess is clipped and then the peacock herl is again wound a couple more turns to form a divided body.

I've listed but a handful of the wet flies you can tie with the methods you've acquired, just to show you how broad your fly-tying base has become.

# 6 BLACK-NOSE DACE AND BLACK & WHITE MARABOU
## Two Popular Baitfish Patterns

THE WORDS BUCKTAIL and streamer are often used interchangeably, though most fly tiers prefer to think of the bucktail as a baitfish imitation which has a wing made of hair fibers from such materials as deer tail, calf tail, black bear, and similar hairs. The streamer fly, which imitates a baitfish, has a wing that consists primarily of feathers. In this section we are going to tie both a bucktail and a streamer; simple flies, yet two of the most effective patterns in their category.

We will begin with the Black-nose Dace, a pattern designed by Art Flick, to imitate one of the numerous baitfish upon which trout and other fish feed. Its original description calls for the use of polar-bear hair. However, we will substitute calf tail, since the polar bear is now a protected species.

Before we begin, let's take a look at the pattern description and go over some of the materials you will use here.

| BLACK-NOSE DACE | |
|---|---|
| (sizes 4-12) | |
| Hook: | Streamer hook (6XL) |
| Thread: | Black |
| Tail: | Red wool, tied short |
| Rib: | Oval silver tinsel |
| Body: | Flat silver tinsel |
| Wing: | White calf tail over black bear hair over natural brown deer tail (bucktail) |
| Head: | Lacquered black |

**Hook**: Choose a 6XL streamer hook (Mustad model 9575). This model is different from other streamer hooks because it has a loop eye—the eye is formed by looping the metal shank back on itself so the end of the hook wire, for a short distance, is parallel with the shank itself. This gives the hook a short platform just behind the eye which permits easier positioning of materials at that point. A loop eye, unlike a ring eye, will never cut a leader.

**Red wool**: You can buy carded wool yarn in all fly shops, or, if someone in the house is knitting a red sweater, help yourself to a few inches.

**Tinsel**: This is another common item in fly shops. Flat tinsel is usually available in metallic or Mylar form, which one you use is not critical. The metallic is just a little heavier than the Mylar, and its weight will help your fly to get deep when fishing. The disadvantages of most metallic tinsels are that they tarnish unless they are manufactured with a protective coating, and they kink and break if handled improperly. Mylar, while not as strong, is easier to handle and, because it's thinner, it can also be used as shoulders or lateral lines on baitfish imitations by simply tying it in and allowing it to lie rearward. Mylar is usually made with silver on one side and gold on the other, so you get two colors for the price of one. Since we will be tying on a number 6 hook, you want medium flat silver tinsel, and fine oval tinsel.

Oval tinsel is manufactured using a fine tinsel wrapped around a core of cotton or other material. Adding oval tinsel to your fly creates more flash which attracts more attention and that can result in more strikes. You can save one step of the process by using embossed tinsel, which gives a similar effect. However, I recommend that you tie this fly as described in the following procedures, since it will add one more technique to your fly-tying skills.

**Calf tail**: Try to select a tail that has fairly straight fibers, at least one and a half inches long. Some calf tails have hairs that are kinky or curly, so you may have to check through a few packages to find one that is suitable. Also make sure that the tips of the hairs are nicely tapered, not broken or blunted.

**Black bear hair**: You want hair that is shiny black, not too stiff, is fairly straight, and tapers to a fine tip. Some black bears have a brownish tinge and hair this color should not be used in this pattern. You'll also find some hair that has curled, especially if it has been cut from under the legs of the animal. Avoid this type of hair. Again, you'll have to check through the dealer's supply to find the appropriate piece.

**Natural-brown bucktail**: This brown shade is found on the back

1 Lash the red wool to the shank

side of a whitetail deer's tail. Some tails, however, tend to run too dark. In some instances it's almost black, while others have hairs that are tan, not brown. You want a nice medium shade of brown for this pattern. All bucktails (which, incidentally, come from both bucks and does) are sold featuring the white hair. You'll have to check the back of the package for the brown hair, and make sure it's not too wavy.

Let's tie the fly. Clamp a size 6 hook in your vise and spiral the thread onto the hook shank, beginning behind the eye and winding to the bend. Cut a two-inch section of two-strand wool. (Wool is manufactured in single, double, and quadruple strands.)

Place the wool on top of the hook

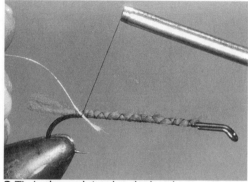

2 Tie in the oval tinsel at the bend

shank with one end reaching to the end of the looped hook eye. Wind your thread forward over the wool and the shank and then back to the bend. By securing the wool along the top of the entire hook shank, you have established a base on which to later wind your tinsel. If you had tied in the wool only near the bend, that area would have more bulk than the rest of the shank and when the tinsel was later wound, you would have a slight lump.

Cut the wool that extends beyond the bend to form a stubby tail measuring half the hook-gape width.

Unwind and cut off a five-inch length of fine oval silver tinsel. Strip a quarter inch of tinsel from its cotton (or other) core, using your thumb and fingernail or a pair of partially

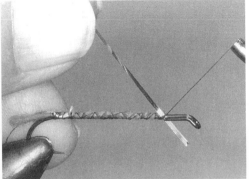

**3** Tie the flat silver tinsel to the shank

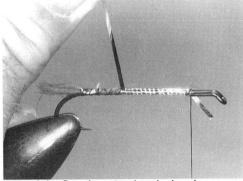

**4** Wind the flat silver tinsel to the bend

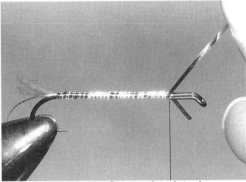

**5** Finish winding the flat tinsel and tie down

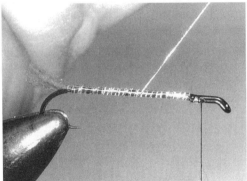

**6** Wind the oval tinsel forward in open wraps

closed scissors. Place the cotton core against the hook shank, with its end pointing diagonally downward between the hook shank and tying thread. Tie down the core and cover it completely with thread wraps so only the tinsel shows when it is later wrapped over the flat tinsel.

Bring your thread forward to a position where the return wire of the looped eye terminates.

Cut a nine- to ten-inch length of medium flat silver tinsel. Place one end against the hook shank pointing diagonally downward as shown.

Take five turns of thread around the tinsel, securing it firmly to the hook. Let the bobbin hang in place. Grasp the tinsel and wind it around the hook shank in adjoining turns to the bend—the turns should not overlap. When you reach the bend, cover all of the cotton core of the oval tinsel. Then reverse the tinsel and wind it in adjoining turns forward to the tying thread. (The tinsel is wound over itself as you work forward.)

Before you make your last turn of tinsel and just before it has reached the thread, hold the tinsel firmly and tightly between your left thumb and forefinger in a vertical position and undo the previous five turns of thread. After unwinding the five turns of thread, wind the tinsel (still held between your left thumb and forefinger) one final turn around the shank. You are actually using the tinsel to tie itself down, and you are reducing bulk by eliminating unnecessary winds.

Wind the thread around the tinsel again, securing it to the shank. Five or six turns should do it. When the tinsel is locked in tightly, cut away both excess ends and cover any exposed bits with one layer of thread for a smooth finish.

This procedure eliminates any unnecessary bulk from the head of the fly. This is important, because we will be using three different hair fibers to form the wing, and the less

**7** Separate the hair fibers

**8** Measure the calftail fibers for length

**9** Tie in the hair and cut the butt ends

material and thread under the head, the neater it will be. Your thread should not be resting at the rear of the looped eye platform.

Grasp the oval tinsel tied in earlier and wind it forward to the thread in an open spiral. The spiral is spaced so there are approximately six wraps of oval tinsel around the flat tinsel. (If you end up with five or seven, it's not critical.) When you wind the oval tinsel forward, keep it tight so it doesn't hang loose from the body.

Upon reaching the thread, tie the oval tinsel to the shank just underneath the end of the loop-eye platform. By tying it to the shank on the underside, the top of the platform remains smooth and even for the construction of the wing.

Separate a bunch of fibers from the rest of the hair on the white calf tail, and cut them free as close to the skin as possible. Try to keep the tips aligned as you cut. The thickness of the bunch of fibers, when compressed, should be approximately that of a round toothpick. (There were 59 fibers in the bunch I used for this demonstration. This is only an approximate guide, since some tails have finer, or heavier fibers than others. Still, it should be of some help.)

To further even up the hair, hold the bunch by the tips and pull and tease the shorter fibers (and any fuzz) from the butt ends. This eliminates the short hairs from the bunch. Most animals have hair or fur of varying length growing from their skin. (Shedding of fur and hair during seasonal changes results in a constant new supply growing in, and these are shorter than established hairs.)

When you've removed the shorter hairs, grasp those that protrude beyond the rest at the tips, pull them out of the bunch, and realign them so all the tips are even. If your calftail fibers are fairly straight and not kinky or curly, you can insert them, tips down, in a hair stacker (sold in fly shops), or use a lipstick tube or empty cartridge casing. Tapping the stacker on the table causes the tips to slide, settle, and align themselves.

When the tips are fairly even (they don't have to be absolutely perfect, in fact, a slight tapering is desirable) measure the bunch along the top of the hook shank so the tips extend past the bend by half of a shank length. Before you tie the hair

**10** Apply a coat of head cement

**11** Measure the black-bear hair

**12** Tie in the hair and trim it at an angle

to the shank, coat the platform area (the top of the looped eye) with head cement. (To make the platform tacky, I apply clear nail polish, using the brush in the jar. It's easier than trying to apply head cement with a dubbing needle.)

Having measured the calf-tail fibers for proper length, transfer the bunch to your left thumb and forefinger and lash it to the doubled platform of hook shank. (You should now be familiar with the technique of passing the thread between thumb and finger pads to secure a material to the shank.) Four or five turns of thread should do the job.

With your scissors, cut away the excess fibers that protrude beyond the eye. However, as you make the cut, angle your scissors so that the hairs are cut at a slant. (If you cut the excess fibers straight up and down, you will form a ledge, and create an unnatural foundation for forming the head.)

The trimmed ends of the calf tail should extend right up to the eye, but not into it. Take a few more turns of thread to cover any exposed ends and to keep the platform level. (Use as few turns of thread as possible to accomplish this. Remember, we want to avoid all unnecessary bulk.) Coat the platform once more with cement or nail polish.

Measure the bunch against the calf tail so that when they are tied in, the tips of the black bear and calf tail will be even.

Tie the black bear to the shank directly on top of the calf tail fibers at the center of the platform.

Trim the excess fibers (using the angled scissor cut) protruding beyond the hook eye at a point about $1/32$ inch behind where you trimmed the calf tail. You are creating a stepped effect so when the head is formed, it will have a taper. Smooth the area with a minimum number of turns of thread and apply a thin coat of cement.

Cut an equal-size bundle of brown bucktail fibers and align the tips. Measure the bunch along the top of the black bear, so that when it is tied in, the tips of all three types of hair are aligned.

Tie the bucktail to the hook shank directly on top of the black bear, slightly to the rear of the center of the platform.

Trim the butts (slanting the scissors as before) at a point $1/32$ of an inch behind where you trimmed the

**13** Measure the natural brown bucktail

**14** Tie in and trim the bucktail fibers

**15** Form the thread with tying thread

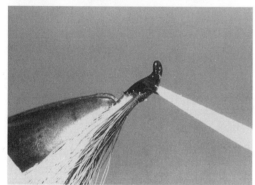

**16** Paint the head with black lacquer

**17** Black-nose Dace

black bear hair. This is the last step in the stepped effect.

Place a drop of head cement on the butt ends of the deer hair before you begin to wind thread to form the head. Cementing the head now will help prevent the hair from slipping.

Forming the head is not difficult. It is simply a matter of winding the thread so it fills any hollows, smooths out bumps, and results in a neatly tapered, cone-shape head. Begin by winding over areas with exposed butts or other material and then gradually work the thread back and forth to establish the taper. The idea is to build a head that is shaped like the head of a natural baitfish.

Don't be concerned if the head on your fly turns out too large. During your first few attempts the heads you make may be too large, but with a little effort you'll improve with each succeeding fly. You'll find that using a little less hair in the wing, a few less turns of thread, or trimming the bunches of hair more accurately will result in a neater appearance. For this fly, we used fine thread because heavy thread builds large, ungainly heads.

Some fly tiers use thicker bunches of hair, which may result in a fuller, and, perhaps, a prettier wing. Unfortunately, the price paid for this enhancement is a large bulky head and a fly that will not sink deep enough to get down to the fish. It is better to be on the sparse side than to overload the wing.

When the head of your fly is complete, apply a whip-finish knot or half hitch the thread. For a shiny black head, use two or three coats of head lacquer. The first coat is usually absorbed into the thread windings.

Next, we'll tie what is known as a streamer pattern. I've selected the Black and White Marabou streamer, which is one of the easiest of all streamers to tie, and also one of the most effective.

| BLACK & WHITE MARABOU STREAMER (sizes 4-12) | |
|---|---|
| Hook: | Streamer (6XL) |
| Thread: | Black 6/0 |
| Body: | Flat silver tinsel |
| Wing: | Black marabou over white marabou |
| Head: | Black |

Clamp a size 6 hook in your vise and attach your thread to the shank just behind the eye. Wind the thread to the end of the looped-eye platform.

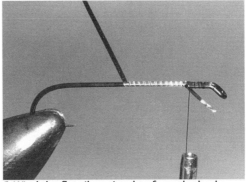

**1** Wind the flat silver tinsel to form the body

Tie in a ten-inch section of flat silver tinsel (or Mylar) and wind it in adjoining turns to the bend, then back again to the tie-in point – exactly like you did for the body of the Black-nose Dace.

For the wing, use marabou "shorts," which were explained in the tying instructions for the Woolly Bugger. The short, or blood, feathers are ideal for this pattern.

Remove any fluff or short fibers from the base of the white marabou feather. Measure the marabou along the top of the hook shank, so the tips extend half a shank length past the bend when the feather is tied in.

Tie the marabou feather on top of the platform formed by the looped portion of the hook eye, and trim away the excess. Take enough turns

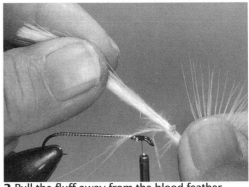

**2** Pull the fluff away from the blood feather

around the butt ends to lash them to the platform from the eye to the end of the doubled shank.

Select a black marabou feather of similar configuration, and measure it against the white marabou so the tips will be aligned when it is tied in.

Tie the black marabou feather directly on top of the white marabou. For a tapered head, cut the excess black marabou about 1/32 of an inch behind where you trimmed the white marabou.

Take enough turns of thread around the head area to form a natural taper that is imitative of a slim baitfish. When you've achieved the proper shape, whip finish the thread and apply the necessary coats of black lacquer for a smooth, shiny head.

**3** Measure the white marabou for length

**4** Measure the black marabou for length

**5** Tie in the black marabou

**6** Black & White Marabou Streamer

After learning a few of the basics for bucktail and streamer tying, you are now equipped to tie the following list of patterns, and perhaps a few designs of your own.

## SQUIRREL TAIL
(sizes 4-10)

| | |
|---|---|
| Hook: | Streamer (6XL) |
| Thread: | Black, 6/0 |
| Rib: | Fine oval silver tinsel |
| Body: | Flat silver tinsel |
| Wing: | A few strands of white calf tail over which a bunch (thickness of a wooden matchstick) of gray squirrel-tail fibers (both half a shank length past bend) |
| Head: | Black with yellow pupil |

Note: After two coats of black lacquer have been applied to the head and allowed to dry, a dubbing needle (or toothpick) is used to paint a yellow eye on each side of the head.

Marabou streamers are tied in a variety of colors with red, white, black, yellow, and olive, or any combination, being the most commonly used. Some marabou streamers have a tail of red hackle and others may sport a beard or shoulder of feathers or other material. Almost every combination is productive. You should choose colors that you personally feel will be the most effective for trout, bass, or other gamefish. Of all the materials you can possibly lash to a hook shank, marabou may just be the deadliest fish taker of all because, when it is in the water, it acts as if it's alive.

**ESOPUS BUCKTAIL**
(sizes 4-12)

| | |
|---|---|
| Hook: | Streamer (6XL) |
| Thread: | Black, 6/0 |
| Tail: | Green calf-tail fibers (gap width past bend) |
| Rib: | Fine flat silver tinsel |
| Body: | Very pale pink dubbing fur |
| Wing: | Sparse bunches of the following from bottom to top White calf tail, pink calf tail, green calf tail, badger fur guard hair fibers (all slightly past end of tail) |

**RYER'S SOCKEYE**
(size 2)

| | |
|---|---|
| Hook: | Streamer (6XL) |
| Thread: | Red, 6/0 |
| Tail: | Red over yellow calf tail (gap width past bend) |
| Rib: | Medium flat silver tinsel |
| Underbody: | Medium lead wire (.024) |
| Body: | Medium orange chenille (size 1) |
| Wing: | Red over yellow bucktail |
| Head: | Red |

This design by Bill Ryer has taken more than its share of sockeye salmon in Alaska. It is also effective on other salmon and steelhead.

**TROUT FIN BUCKTAIL**
(sizes 4-10)

| | |
|---|---|
| Hook: | Streamer (6XL) |
| Thread: | Black, 6/0 |
| Tail: | Red hackle fibers |
| Rib: | Fine oval silver tinsel |
| Body: | Flat silver tinsel |
| Wing: | Sparse white bucktail over which sparse black bucktail over which a bunch of orange bucktail equal in thickness to both white and black bucktail (all half a shank length past bend) |
| Head: | Black |

# 7 DARK HENDRICKSON DRY FLY
## A Model for Many Mayflies

BY THE TIME you arrive at this chapter hopefully your fingers have acquired experience and dexterity and they're not strangers to the movements needed to tie any fly. I've saved the dry fly for last because it is just a shade more difficult than the others, and requires educated fingers to perform the necessary tying techniques. This type of fly, as the name implies, is tied so it will float on the surface of the water.

We'll tie the Dark Hendrickson, which imitates a common species of mayfly. As you read more about the aquatic insects fish feed on, you will find that the the Hendrickson imitates the *Ephemerella subvaria* mayfly, as it is called in Latin. The Hendrickson is tied in various versions, including the "Light Hendrickson," the "Red Quill" (which imitates the gender of the species), and the "Dark Hendrickson." We will tie the Dark Hendrickson, since we already have some of the materials required for its construction.

Except for the hook, which is made of light wire to help the finished fly to float, the ingredients of this pattern should have a familiar

---

**DARK HENDRICKSON**
(sizes 12-14)

| | |
|---|---|
| Hook: | Standard dry fly |
| Thread: | Gray |
| Wing: | Wood-duck flank fibers (or substitute) |
| Tail: | Medium dun hackle fibers |
| Body: | Muskrat dubbing fur |
| Hackle: | Medium dun |

---

ring. The feather used to form the hackle collar must have stiff fibers so it can support the fly on the water's surface. Let's take a closer look at the dry-fly hackle.

The requirements for a rooster feather used to collar a dry fly are: stiffness, size, and lustre. Years ago, when most of rooster necks were imported, obtaining some hackle sizes and colors, such as dun, was difficult. Today, most necks come from genetically bred birds that are raised to have stiff hackle in sizes that accommodate even the smallest hooks. How can you tell if a hackle is of good quality? Anytime you purchase a rooster neck you should:

1. Check the overall color and lustre of the feathers. Dull necks do not reflect light as well as shiny ones, and generally they are of poor quality.

2. Separate one of the feathers near the upper half of the neck from its neighbors (do not pluck it from the neck) and bend it in an arc so the fibers stand out from the main stem so you can see how long or short they are. Pick out another feather even higher on the neck and check the fiber length in this area. A good neck should have more than two gross of feathers capable of collaring hook sizes from 12 to 20. (More on size later.)

3. While you have one feather isolated from the others, see how well the fibers stand erect from the main stem. They should protrude from the stem rather firmly, and not lean or bend.

Another method for checking stiffness is to bend the neck in a shallow arc and brush your fingertips back and forth across the feathers. Do they bounce back to their original position quickly or are they limp and slushy in their movements? Those that bounce, vibrate, and quiver generally have high-quality hackle fibers.

Don't worry if you don't understand all the nuances of hackle quality at the outset. It will come to you gradually as you become a more experienced fly tier. Barb stiffness in a dry-fly hackle helps stand the fly on top of the water (using the water's surface tension to keep the fly floating). Soft hackle will collapse under the weight of the fly, allowing the body of the fly to come in contact with the water, causing it to absorb water and sink. Stiff fibers keep the fly's body elevated from the water's surface, preventing water absorption to a degree and keeping the fly "dry" and floating longer. Flies can be impregnated with fly "dope," a waterproofing agent that enhances flotation. Ideally, we try to tie a dry fly using techniques that make flotant unnecessary (but that's a lofty goal—most drys, sooner or later, need to be treated with flotant). If you would like to learn more about hackle, I recommend reading *The Metz Book of Hackle.* Now, let's tie a dry fly.

Wind your thread onto the shank in close wraps, beginning slightly behind the eye and winding rearward ⅛ inch. This forms a thread base upon which the wing can be tied. Bring the thread forward so it rests in the center of the thread base you just formed.

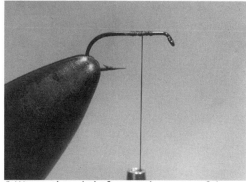

**1** Wrap a thread platform at the center of the shank

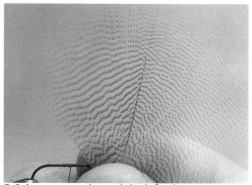

**2** Select a natural wood-duck feather

The wings of a standard dry fly are always tied on first. This is important for two reasons: 1) winging is the most difficult procedure in constructing a dry fly; and 2) the wing determines the proportions for the rest of the fly. The exception to tying the wing on first is any dry fly with a clipped deer-hair body because the wing could easily be clipped off as the body is trimmed.

The wing here is made from the same wood-duck flank fibers used in earlier patterns. Again, if you don't have natural wood duck, use mallard which has been dyed to a wood-duck color. It's a trade-off when selecting one winging material over the other. It is easier to work with the natural, because it is stiffer and easier to handle, but mallard will allow you to

learn the same techniques while using a less expensive material.

Hold a wood-duck feather (or mallard substitute) between your right thumb and forefinger. Notice that the feather is rounded and the tips flow in curve. We need a ¾-inch-wide segment of fibers with the tips aligned.

Hold the feather firmly, and use your left thumb and forefinger to pull and stroke the fibers downward until the tips are even. When the tips are aligned, hold the feather by the tips with your left thumb and forefinger. Let go with your right thumb and forefinger. Cut the section from the stem as close to the stem as possible.

You should now be holding an evenly aligned section of fibers

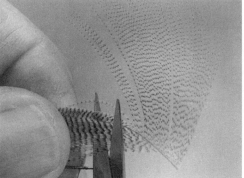

**3** Pull the fibers down until the tips are aligned

**4** Hold the tips evenly and cut the feather

**5** Measure the fibers for wing height

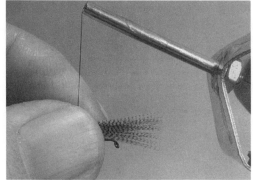

**6** Hold the clump in position to tie in

between left thumb and forefinger. Now we must compact these fibers into a single clump. With your right thumb and forefinger, squeeze the base and lower portion (those protruding from between left thumb and forefinger) of the fibers together. Open your left thumb and forefinger, releasing the tips, and then use your left thumb and forefinger to compress the tips once more. You are manipulating the fibers between your left and right hands to form a single clump.

Hold the base of the clump between your left thumb and forefinger, and (with the aid of a pair of tweezers) reposition the fibers so the tips protrude and point straight out from between your left thumb and forefinger. Once you get the clump into this position, it can be measured against the hook shank and tied on.

Hold the clump of fibers directly over the hook shank. Rest your left thumb and forefinger directly over the bend of the hook with the tips of the fibers pointing at the hook eye. Position the clump of fibers so the tips are exactly even with the eye of the hook. Look at the clump and determine which point on the clump is above the bend. Make the height of the wing equal to the length of the hook shank from bend to eye. This proportion applies to hooks with standard-length shanks.

Now, move your thumb and forefinger forward, so the portion that was over the bend is now directly over the center of the thread base at the middle of the shank.

Bring the thread up against the pad of your thumb, over the fibers, down against your finger pad, under and around the hook shank and upward again. Repeat the maneuver. (By now, you should be getting familiar with this "soft-loop" technique.) Pull straight up on the tying thread. By pulling straight up as opposed to down on the far side,

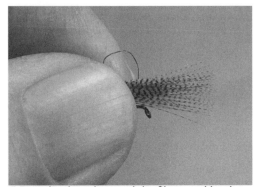

**7** Pass the thread around the fibers and hook

**8** Wood-duck fibers tied in

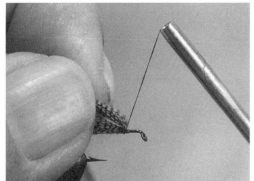

**9** Pull tips back, wind thread against the base

**10** Fibers forced up by thread wraps

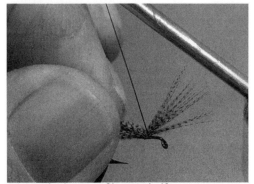

**11** Divide the wing fibers in half

you snug the thread directly down on the material instead of rolling the material around the shank and off to the back side.)

Take two or three more turns of thread around the same area to secure the fibers to the shank.

With your left thumb and forefinger, lift the clump to a vertical posi-

tion and hold it there. Take three or four turns of thread in front of, and slightly against, the base of the clump. This procedure props up the clump so it stands away from the hook shank.

Now it's time to split the clump into two equal sections. Divide the clump approximately in half, using

your fingers. Pull the half nearest you away from the other.

While holding the two halves apart, bring the thread through the division from front to rear. Allow the thread to hang behind the wing fibers on the far side of the shank. This simple move should hold the two sections slightly apart.

Now grasp the section of fibers on the far side of the hook shank and hold them away as you bring your thread under the shank and through the two clumps from rear to front. This should separate the two sections a little more. Allow the thread to hang on the far side of the shank in front of the wing. You are making a simple figure-eight crisscross with your thread to separate the two sections of the wing.

**12** Pass the thread between the sections

**13** The wing fibers divided into two sections

**14** Encircle half of the fibers with thread

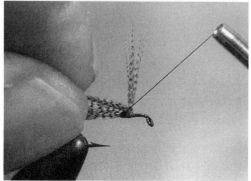

**15** Now encircle the other half with thread

**16** Move the thread to the rear between wings

Bring the thread through the division once more from front to rear. Now wind two turns of thread around the hook shank directly in back of the wings.

At this point the wood-duck fibers are beginning to resemble an upright, divided wing, although they are still a bit scraggly and some of the fibers are misbehaving. So far, we've brought the thread between the two sections of fibers to create a division. Next, we will encircle the base of the fibers with thread, so the thread completely surrounds the fibers in each section and compacts them at the base.

Bring the thread, on a horizontal plane, around the base of the far section of fibers for one full turn. Continue around the base of these fibers a second time. Bring the thread through the divided fibers from front to rear and then under the hook shank and once completely around the hook shank directly in back of the wings.

Continue with the thread, on a horizontal plane, completely around the base of the fibers nearest you. Continue around the base of these fibers for one more turn and bring the thread through the division of fibers from front to rear. Wind two turns of thread around the hook shank in back of the wings.

Take a break. The winging of dry flies is one of the toughest procedures in fly tying. I didn't mention it

**17** Finish wrapping the thread behind the wing

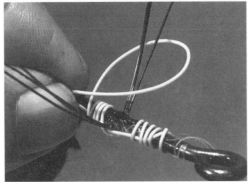

**18** Encircle one wing half with thread

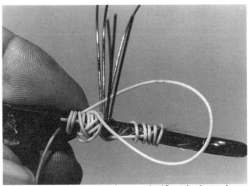

**19** Encircle the second wing half with thread

**20** Trim some butts short

**21** Trim the remaining butts longer

earlier because I didn't want to discourage you. Now that you have the hang of it, it will get easier and easier as you go along. This is the toughest procedure – everything after this is downhill.

To help you understand the procedure more clearly I've used a fly line and a very large hook while Matty took the photographs. You can use this type of arrangement yourself, if you wish, just to get the hang of the curves and turns of thread.

You will find, as I have, that it requires certain pressure with the thread and your fingers to make the thread behave against the wispy wood-duck fibers. But a little practice will take you a long way.

If, for some reason, the wing doesn't sit up the way it should, take it off and try another. Practicing these maneuvers while the process is fresh in your mind will lock it in your memory.

The next step is to trim the excess wood-duck butts. Don't simply cut them away behind the wings. Cut half of them behind the wing, half of the remaining fibers near the center of the hook shank, and the rest of the fibers just before the bend. Using this stagger-cut method creates a tapered underbody that will make it easier to form a neatly dubbed fur body.

Wind the thread over the trimmed butts to the bend, smoothing out the underbody as you go. Then wind for-

**22** Form a tapered underbody with thread

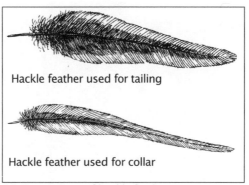

Hackle feather used for tailing

Hackle feather used for collar

**23** Comparison of hackle feathers

ward to a point one-third of the shank length forward of the bend.

Next tie in rooster hackle fibers to form a supporting tail. First, a few words on the tailing material are in order.

Most rooster necks have a limited supply of feathers with fibers long enough to support a size 10 or 12 fly. So, when you select a feather for tailing, always choose one with fiber length that best matches the particular size of fly that you are tying. For example, if you are tailing a size 16 dry fly, do not use a feather with tailing fibers longer than necessary for this size fly. Why waste long tailing material on a smaller fly when hackles with long fibers are in short supply?

For tailing material you need a blue-dun (or bronze-dun) feather which has a fiber length, from the webby portion to the tip, slightly longer than the length of the hook shank from the eye to the bend.

Before going on, let me try to clear up some confusion that has come from one of fly-tying's hackle misnomers. You will see references made in other publications that this pattern (and many others) has tails and a hackle collar made of "blue-dun" hackle. Don't let the words fool you. There is no blue in blue dun—it is a shade of gray. When you see a reference to "bronze dun," it means that the feather is gray with a bronze or brownish cast. I prefer a medium bronze-gray tone for the collar and tail of this pattern. But don't worry too much about color. As you

advance in fly tying and fishing, you'll learn that color means different things to different tiers (and also to the trout) and there will always be a certain amount of confusion and disagreement about it.

Isolate one of the larger feathers that grows from the side of the cape. Stroke the fibers downward, so they stand out, and check their length. To determine if the size is correct for your fly, measure the fibers against the shank of the hook. The portion of fiber beyond the web should be slightly longer than the shank of the hook.

When you've chosen the proper feather, pluck it from the neck. Grasp the feather by the tip and stroke the fibers downward so they extend at right angles from the stem.

Making sure the tip ends of the fibers are evenly aligned, grasp a ½-inch section of them by their tips with your left thumb and forefinger. Squeeze the fibers firmly so you won't lose your grip. Squeeze! Then pull the stem away from the fibers. (Don't try to pull the fibers from the feather – this will misalign them. Pull the feather from the fibers.)

Use your right thumb and forefinger to squeeze the fibers into a single clump while releasing your grip

24 Stroke the fibers straight out from the stem

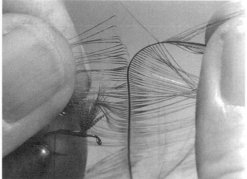

25 Align the tips and strip them from the stem

26 Measure the fibers for tail length

27 Tie in the hackle fibers to form the tail

with your left hand. Measure these tail fibers for length, which is equal to the length of the hook shank or the wing height. Transfer the fibers to your left hand, by holding the tips between your left thumb and forefinger. Be careful to keep the tips aligned.

Place the fibers on top of and slightly to the front side of the hook shank. Take one turn of thread around them. Pull the thread toward you (this prevents the fibers from being pulled down the far side), and remove your left thumb and forefinger. Check the tail length. It should be equal to the length of the hook shank. If not, unwind the one turn of thread and reposition the fibers so they are the correct length. Take two more thread wraps to secure the clump and trim the excess butts.

With the tail fibers in position, wind the thread to the bend, but no further because this will force the fibers down the curve of the bend. Then wrap the thread back to a position just slightly to the rear of the center of the shank.

Take a break. The next step is to tie in the body of the fly.

The process for constructing the body is exactly the same as the one used to make the body of the Dark Hendrickson nymph. So, use the same technique to dub muskrat fur onto the thread, and wind the dubbing in an increasing diameter to a point approximately 1/16 inch behind the base of the wings. Now you can tie in the hackle, which will form the supportive collar on this fly.

## THE HACKLE

For a size 12 hook you need two hackles from a natural or dyed dun rooster neck. The fibers growing from the center stem should have a length three-quarters of the wing

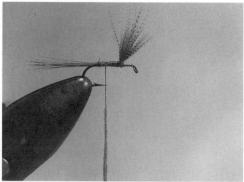

**28** Spin muskrat dubbing onto the thread

**29** Wind the dubbed thread to form the body

**30** Leave space between the body and wing

**31** Measure hackle for proper height

**32** Trim the hackle butt fibers

height (or three-quarters of the hook shank length). You will have to search for the correct hackle size, but generally, on a genetic neck, these feathers exist at a point approximately a third of the way down from the nape, or tip, of the neck. You can isolate one of the feathers on the neck and measure the

hackle against the wing by bending the feather in an arc around the hook shank.

When you have plucked two hackles, determine where the webby portion of the feather ends. Tie the feather to the shank from this portion upward, toward the tip of the feather. (You can use part of the

webby hackle if the overall feather is too short.)

Trim the fibers from the stem below the point where it will be tied to the stem.

Don't pull the fibers from the stem, because stripping them will make the center stem smooth and slick, causing possible slippage or twisting when the hackle is wound around the shank. Cut the excess butts of the feathers, leaving only about ⅛ inch of trimmed butts on the hackle.

With the shiny side of both feathers facing you, place them against the hook shank so the trimmed butts extend diagonally downward from behind the wings and between the hook shank and thread. The butts should point forward, toward the hook eye.

**33** Properly prepare the hackle butt stems

**34** Tie in the hackle stems behind the wings

**35** Tie the hackle stems to the shank

**36** Attach the pliers and lift the first hackle

**37** Swing the hackle down and to the right

Wind two turns of thread around the hackle stems behind the wings and two turns around them in front of the wings, securing them firmly to the shank.

Grasp the tip of one of these hackles in the jaws of your hackle pliers. Make sure it is gripped securely. Swing the hackle upward with your pliers, around the top of the hook shank and down the other side. Observe the individual hackle fibers. Are they standing erect from the hook shank at a 90-degree angle? If so, good. If, however, they tend to lie rearward, swing the hackle pliers toward the eye and then straight down. This trick usually aligns them.

Wind the first hackle around the hook shank in back of the wings (one turn in front of the other) for three turns, and wind three more turns of hackle around the shank in front of the wings. If the wing gets in the way, hold it back with your fingers as the hackle passes it. (It's always a good idea to make the turn directly in back and the turn directly in front of the wings as close to the wings as possible so the completed collar does not have gaps.)

When you've completed the last turn of hackle around the shank, hold the feather up in a vertical position, leaning slightly forward, and bring the thread around the stem to secure it to the shank. Do not cut the excess.

Go back and grasp the second

**38** Bring the first hackle down at an angle

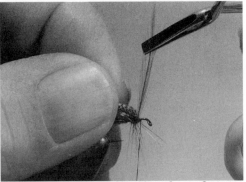

**39** Make three turns of hackle in front of wing

**40** Hold the hackle tip as shown and tie it off

**41** Second hackle tied off near the hook eye

**42** Wind the second hackle between the first

**43** Tie down the second hackle

hackle feather with the pliers and wind it forward as you did the first. This time, wind the feather through and between the fibers of the first hackle.

As you wrap the feather around the shank, give the hackle a slight back-and-forth motion so that the stem of this hackle can settle in between the wraps of the first. Using two feathers results in more fibers, which gives the collar more supportive "feet" on the water when fished.

When the second hackle has been wound forward to the thread, tie it down as you did the first. Now clip both excess hackle tips.

Take another two turns of thread around the shank behind the eye, and then half hitch or whip finish the thread. Do not make turns of thread to build a head of thread. You don't want a bulky head on this fly. In fact, this area should be as clean as possible. Cut away the thread and place a drop of head cement on the thread wraps.

44 Cut away the excess hackle tips

45 Dark Hendrickson

You've just completed your first dry fly. With the knowledge you've gained in tying your first dry fly you can now, without further instructions, tie the following patterns.

## LIGHT HENDRICKSON
(sizes 12-14)

| | |
|---|---|
| Hook: | Standard dry fly |
| Thread: | Gray |
| Wing: | Wood-duck flank fibers |
| Tail: | Medium blue dun or bronze dun hackle fibers |
| Body: | Pinkish-tan fox dubbing |
| Hackle: | Medium blue dun (or bronze dun) |

## DORATO HARE'S EAR
(sizes 10-14)

| | |
|---|---|
| Hook: | Standard dry fly |
| Thread: | Brown |
| Wing: | Wood-duck flank fibers |
| Tail: | Grizzly |
| Body: | Hare's-ear dubbing |
| Hackle: | Dark ginger and grizzly mixed, one of each feather (After completion the hackle is trimmed on top and bottom) |

## GRAY FOX
(sizes 12-14)

| | |
|---|---|
| Hook: | Standard dry fly |
| Thread: | Primrose (yellow) |
| Wing: | Mallard flank fibers |
| Tail: | Golden ginger |
| Body: | Fawn/beige fox dubbing |
| Hackle: | Light shade of grizzly and golden ginger |

## LIGHT CAHILL
(sizes 10-18)

| | |
|---|---|
| Hook: | Standard dry fly |
| Thread: | Yellow |
| Wing: | Wood-duck flank fibers |
| Tail: | Dark cream |
| Body: | Creamy yellow dubbing |
| Hackle: | Dark cream |

## DARK CAHILL
(sizes 12-18)

| | |
|---|---|
| Hook: | Standard dry fly |
| Thread: | Tan, gray, or black |
| Wing: | Wood-duck flank fibers |
| Tail: | Dark ginger |
| Body: | Muskrat dubbing |
| Hackle: | Dark ginger |

Dark ginger is a light reddish-brown color. It is very common.

## MARCH BROWN
(sizes 12-14)

| | |
|---|---|
| Hook: | Standard dry fly |
| Thread: | Orange |
| Wing: | Mallard flank with bronze tinge or well-marked wood-duck flank fibers |
| Tail: | Dark ginger |
| Body: | Sandy-beige dubbing |
| Hackle: | Dark ginger and grizzly mixed |

There are, of course, other dry flies you can tie using the techniques just acquired. This short list, however, should give you the general idea.

## Some Final Comments

A manual of this type can encompass just so much. Through it, you've been presented a multitude of techniques and procedures that you will use as long as you tie flies. What you've learned here will provide the foundation for many future efforts. There are lots of other aspects and techniques you may wish to learn to further expand your knowledge in this wonderful hobby.

For those of you who are so inclined, I suggest you look into some of the books listed in the bibliography, especially *The Complete Book of Fly Tying* and *The Book of Fly Patterns*, and you might become involved with some of the organizations listed. It's important to observe as many fly tiers at work as you can, whenever you can.

Here's to you – and to the good times.

# Bibliography

These books have been selected to assist you by adding to your fly-tying knowledge. Most of them are available at your local fly shop or library. The books are listed alphabetically by author.

Dennis, Jack
*Western Trout Fly Tying Manual*
Snake River Books
Jackson Hole, WY (1974)
The numerous black-and-white photographs showing detailed tying sequences make this book ideal for novice fly tiers. My only difference of opinion with Dennis's fine work is in his approach to the dry fly, in which he does not tie the wings in first. Barring that, a great deal of information can be garnered from this book.

Flick, Art
*Art Flick's New Streamside Guide*
Lyons & Burford
New York, NY (1982)
This compact work by the late Art Flick was first published in 1942, and it concentrates on the fly patterns related to major mayfly emergences of the East and Midwest. It does not include detailed photos showing how the flies are tied, but, nevertheless, it gives much information on these patterns.

Flick, Art
*Art Flick's Master Fly Tying Guide*
Lyons & Burford
New York, NY (1972, 1982)
Here Flick gives us a broad spectrum of various flies with full photographic sequences of how they are tied. This is a compilation by such experts as Dave Whitlock, Ernest Schwiebert, Lefty Kreh, Doug Swisher and Carl Richards, Ed Koch and Ted Niemeyer, each tying their specialty.

Fulsher, Keith, and Charles Krom
*Hairwing Atlantic Salmon Flies*
Fly Tyer, Inc.
North Conway, NH
For those interested in tying patterns for Atlantic salmon, this book is a must. Fulsher and Krom give detailed tying instructions, and the most effective patterns are featured on four-color plates.

Harder, John
*The Index of Orvis Fly Patterns*
The Orvis Company
Manchester, VT (1978)
This book, which is presented in a ring binder, was compiled and edited by John Harder, and it lists all the Orvis patterns and other flies. For some patterns, fly-tying instructions are included. Each fly is featured in full color. This is a reference work that should be in every fly tier's library.

Leiser, Eric
*The Book of Fly Patterns*
Alfred A. Knopf
New York, NY (1987)

I may be prejudiced, but I have yet to find another single book that I think contains as much information for the fly tier as this one. I scoured every catalog and researched every book available in addition to obtaining the assistance of key experts such as Lefty Kreh, John Harder, Dick Stewart, Keith Fulsher, Charlie Krom, the Dettes and many others to make this as complete and useful as possible. There are over 1,000 patterns listed, with 500 photos and illustrations relating to the patterns, including techniques and processes necessary for each pattern. There are twelve color plates of flies tied, in most cases, by their creators or other experts. It also features sections listing where hard-to-find materials may be obtained, substitutes for rare materials, a list of suppliers, a full bibliography, and a glossary. This one is a "must" if you tie flies.

Leiser, Eric
*Fly Tying Materials*
Lyons & Burford
New York, NY (1982)

Contains chapters on tools, hooks, materials and how to use them. Sections concerning collecting, preserving and dyeing and many other areas important to the fly tier are included.

Leiser, Eric
*The Metz Book of Hackle*
Lyons & Burford
New York, NY (1986)

This book specializes in the feathers of the common chicken. How to determine quality, the protection of feathers, dyeing, and many tips concerning mixing and blending of hackle to save money.

Leiser, Eric
*The Complete Book of Fly Tying*
Alfred A. Knopf
New York, NY (1977)

While there is no such thing as a "complete" book on any subject, this volume is as close to it as I could get. It has detailed tying instructions for both the beginner and advanced devotee, whether fishing in freshwater or saltwater. Now in its eleventh printing, it is being used as a teaching aide by many instructors of fly-tying classes.

Rosborough, E. H. "Polly"
*Tying and Fishing the Fuzzy Nymphs*
Stackpole Books
Harrisburg, PA (1978)

This is a small book with limited patterns. However, the techniques described here and the flies, all of which are fuzzy, are important if you want to tie flies that take fish.

Shaw, Helen
*Fly Tying*
Wylie
New York, NY (1981)

This is a beginner's book. While it does not contain any fly patterns, it does, through photographic sequence, teach technique.

Stewart, Dick
*Universal Fly Tying Guide*
Stephen Greene Press
Brattleboro, VT (1979)

This is a basic fly-pattern reference. There are approximately 140 patterns and a full-color section of the materials used. A tying section showing how to tie dry, wet, nymph, and streamer flies is also included.

## PERIODICALS

*American Angler*
P.O. Box 4100
Bennington, VT 05201
(802) 447-1518

This handsome, bi-monthly which saw its birth almost eighteen years ago as *Fly Tyer* magazine, now covers all aspects of fly fishing while retaining its primary thrust in the world of fly tying. There is much value here for the fly tier. Abenaki Publishers, Inc., the publisher of *American Angler* and this book, also markets a line of fly-fishing and fly-tying books.

*Flyfishing*
P.O. Box 82112
Portland, OR 97282
(503) 653-8108

Printed five times a year, mostly during cabin-fever season, this loaded-with-information periodical contains numerous items of interest to the fly tier. The publisher also carries a full line of fly-fishing and fly-tying books, which are often featured and advertised in these pages.

*Fly Fisherman*
P.O. Box 8200
Harrisburg, PA 17105
(717) 657-9555

Founded over twenty-five years ago, this bi-monthly, as far as I know, is the oldest magazine in our sport. It carries feature articles by the experts in both fly fishing and fly tying, as well as a regular column entitled "Fly Tier's Bench."

*Fly Rod & Reel*
P.O. Box 370
Camden, ME 04843
(207) 594-9544

Life for this magazine began as *Rod & Reel*, and in the past few years it has changed to a strictly fly-fishing periodical, published bi-monthly.

## ORGANIZATIONS

Here is a list of organizations which can be helpful to you as a fly tier. Membership dues are very reasonable.

FEDERATION OF FLY FISHERS
P.O. Box 1595
Bozeman, MT 59771
(406) 585-7592

This organization is devoted to the promotion of fly fishing in clean, pure waters. It has numerous chapters throughout the country, many of which offer fly-fishing and fly-tying classes. A call or postcard will direct you to the nearest chapter. A quarterly magazine, *The Flyfisher*, is included in membership in the FFF.

TROUT UNLIMITED
1500 Wilson Blvd.
Arlington, VA 22209
(703) 522-0200

The primary objective of this group is to protect and preserve the waters in which trout live, and to reclaim polluted waters and restore them to a pristine quality so fish and aquatic insects will survive. TU has numerous chapters, here and abroad, which teach fly fishing and fly tying. Being associated with members of this organization will take you far in your new hobby. A quarterly magazine, *Trout*, is part of membership.

UNITED FLY TYERS, INC.
P.O. Box 220
Maynard, MA 01754

This club's sole purpose is the teaching and preservation of fly tying. The UFT has been with us for over thirty years. Its quarterly magazine contains many innovative tips on tying. Unfortunately, the UFT does not have chapters and, unless you live in the Boston area, you will have to learn from their periodical. However, it's a worthwhile investment. (I admit that I've known some members to travel over a hundred miles just to attend a meeting.)

# Glossary

The definition of certain words, terms or procedures in the following glossary should help you understand fly-tying language in relation to the procedures and methods outlined in this book and many others. As you progress with this engrossing hobby, the following explanations will be quite useful.

## A

**Abdomen**: Usually used in relation to nymph tying, abdomen refers to the posterior body (as separate from the thorax or chest).

**Antennae**: (See Feelers)

**Aftershaft**: A soft, narrow downy feather, growing from the base of the stem of a body feather on birds or chickens. It is sometimes referred to as a philo plume.

## B

**Barb, Barbules**: In fly tying, barb generally refers to the individual fiber growing from the stem of a feather. Barbules are tiny hook-like projections that grow from barbs and keep the fibers locked together. These barbules act something like Velcro®, and this property is employed by full-dress salmon-fly tiers when "marrying" like or unlike feathers to form a wing.

**Beard**: This term is often used interchangeably to refer to a throat or a wet-fly collar. It is simply a material, feather or fur, tied on the underside of the shank, behind the head, to imitate feelers, legs, or other breathing parts of an imitation.

**Blend**: Usually refers to the underfur of an animal which has been intertwined or intermingled with itself, or with another fur for a certain color of dubbing. In recent years, it has also been applied to synthetic furs. Some of the trade names you may encounter are: Natureblend, Hare's Ear Blend, Fly-Rite, Seal's Fur Blend, etc.

**Body**: Refers to the portion of an imitation that covers the hook shank from bend to head. In nymphs, this body is generally broken up into two parts, the abdomen and thorax. In dry flies, it is the portion up to the wing.

**Body Material**: Any natural or synthetic material tied to the shank of the hook between the bend and the head.

**Bullet-shaped**: Refers to the shape of the head, usually in relation to bass bugs, particularly where cork bodies or clipped deer hair are employed.

**Butt**: Used mostly in salmon fly terminology. A butt is usually a piece of herl (peacock or ostrich), floss, or other material tied around the shank before the bend and between the tag, tip, or tail and the body.

## C

**Cheeks**: The term is used in salmon and streamer fly tying and refers to a feather (usually real jungle cock or an imitation), tied in behind the head on each side of the fly, that extends rearward for a short distance (usually over a shoulder feather) along the sides of the fly. A good example would be the Gray Ghost pattern, which calls for cheeks of jungle-cock "eye" feathers.

**Clipped Body**: This body type is formed by spinning deer, antelope, elk, or other hollow hair around the hook shank and trimming it to a body shape with scissors or a razor blade.

**Clump**: A bunch or group of fibers of any material which is tied in as a unit to form a wing

**Collar**: Usually made of various types of hackle, a collar of a fly is tied in behind the head, either as a support for a dry fly or as an imitation of legs on a wet fly or nymph. Salmon and streamer flies are also occasionally "collared" to add more breathing action to the pattern.

**Counter wind, Counter wrap**: Denotes a ribbing-type material, usually thread, floss, or wire which is wound in a counterclockwise direction around the body of a fly.

**Cut Wing**: A feather that has been formed to the shape of an insect's wing by scissors, a razor blade, wing burner, or another type of wing-forming tool.

**D**

**Deer Body**: A fly body constructed of deer hair, usually spun and trimmed.

**Delta Wing**: Rooster or hen-hackle tips tied to the top of the hook shank and protruding rearward at a 45-degree angle. Used mostly in adult-caddis imitations.

**Divided Wing**: Sometimes called an upright divided wing, this term applies to dry-fly wings, usually made of feather (such as wood duck, mallard, or teal), tied in as a unit and divided into two distinct sections with crisscross thread wraps. Usually used to imitate the upright wings of a mayfly.

**Downwing**: Winging material that is tied so that it lies flat over the hook shank is called a downwing. Adult caddis are usually tied with this style of wing.

**Dub, Dubbing**: Dubbing is any material, but usually fur, which can be spun on thread or trapped in a thread loop to form the body of the fly. Thread is dubbed when body material is applied to it. Wrapping dubbed thread around the hook shank forms a dubbed body.

**Dubbing Noodle**: A body material formed by twisting fur or hair in a dubbing loop. It is used especially when coarse materials such as seal fur, hare's-ear fur, and comparable synthetics are called for as bodies.

**Dubbing Loop**: A loop of tying thread into which coarse dubbing or other materials are inserted. The loop is then spun tightly to form the dubbing noodle used to make the body.

**Dun**: In entomology, the adult mayfly. In fly-tying lingo, dun is also a color: an elusive shade of gray that imitates the hue of the wings of many mayflies.

**E**

**Egg Sac**: A small, often colorful sac that holds eggs and is found on the body of ovipositing female mayflies, caddisflies, and other aquatic insects. In fly tying it is usually represented with single turn of chenille or dubbing in the proper color at the end of the abdomen.

**Excess**: Extra material (thread, dubbing, tinsel, hackle) remaining on the hook at the end of each tying step. Excess material is usually clipped away during tying.

**Extended Body**: A fly body that extends beyond the hook shank. Extended bodies are popular for duplicating the larger mayfly species, as well as some stoneflies, grasshoppers, and crickets.

**F**

**Fan Wing**: A style of dry fly that uses white wood-duck breast feathers to form the wing. The Fan-Wing Royal Coachman was one of the more popular patterns of this type some thirty years ago. Fan-wing flies are not popular today.

**Feelers**: Another word for antennae. Feelers on flies are usually made of a firm-yet-flexible material, tied to protrude beyond the head of the fly like the insect's antennae. Goose biots are often used for this purpose.

**Fiber**: An individual piece of hair or hackle is called a fiber. Fibers can be used individually or in clumps to form different parts of a fly. For example, a bunch of deer-tail fibers are used in the make-up of a bucktail wing.

**Flat Wing**: Similar to a downwing. A flat wing sits flat along the back of the fly. This is usually a duck or turkey-wing quill (although some synthetic materials are also popular) that is cut to shape and tied over the back of a fly to imitate the silhouette of the adult natural. Caddis, stonefly, and some terrestrial imitations use flat wings.

**Flight Feathers**: The outer, primary feathers of birds. The flight feathers of ducks, turkey, and geese are examples of some of those used in fly tying.

**Flue**: The barb of a feather. Generally refers to a peacock-eyed tail where the longer "flues" are found three to five inches below the "eyed" portion.

**Folded Hackle**: A feather that has its barbs folded so they protrude from only one side of the stem. Folded hackles are primarily used as wet-fly collars.

**Forked Tail**: Also known as a split tail or divided tail, this is a style of tail in which the fibers are separated to imitate the tail of the natural insect. It is used quite commonly in nymph imitations and is popular in some dry flies.

**Fur Rope**: (See Dubbing Noodle)

**G**

**Gills**: These are the fibrous, breathing and moving appendages found on nymphs and larvae. The action is often simulated in flies by the use of such fine materials as ostrich and peacock herl or a coarse fuzzy fur fiber.

**Guard Hair**: The longer, coarser or thicker hairs found on many animals. Guard hair usually grows along with the finer, shorter underfur that is often used as dubbing. Guard hairs are often used for antennae, tailing, and winging on flies. For example, the Mink-wing Caddis uses the guard hair from a mink tail, and the Woodchuck Caddis uses woodchuck guard hair as winging material.

**H**

**Hackle**: Most often, this word refers to the neck feather of a rooster that is used in tying a traditional dry fly. However, hackle also applies to feathers from partridge, grouse, and other upland game birds. Hackle can also refer to materials other than feathers, such as the rubber hackle used for legs on large nymphs and many bass bugs. The word hackle is also used to describe a tying step in the construction of a fly, as in "hackle the fly," which means to wind a feather collar around the shank of the hook, either for support or to simulate legs.

**Hair Wing**: In regard to a dry fly, it is a wing made of deer hair, calf tail or other animal fibers. In salmon-fly tying it refers to the substitution of hair for feathers in the construction of the fly. In general, hair wings are more durable than feather wings

**Herl**: Any feather, usually peacock, on which the barbs or flues are soft and grow from a fairly supple center stem. Ostrich herl is another example.

## M

**Married Wing or Feather**: A wing constructed from multiple strips of different types and/or colors of quills. Used primarily in salmon-fly tying where multi-color wing sections are employed.

**Midge**: In general, any small fly. Midges imitate the tiniest of mayflies, like Tricoptera and many of the dipterans.

## O

**Optic Eye**: A highly visible eye that is either painted onto the head of the fly (usually baitfish patterns) or simulated by the use of beads, glass taxidermy eyes, or doll eyes. Optic eyes can be a single white or yellow dot, or include an iris and a pupil.

**Outrigger**: This word is sometimes used to describe a forked tail. See Forked Tail.

## P

**Pair, Paired**: Materials that are matched to form symmetrical right and left parts, as in paired quill wings.

**Palmer**: Any material, usually a hackle feather, that is wound around the hook shank or over a completed body in connecting or slightly open turns is said to be palmering. The Woolly Bugger and the the Brown Bivisible dry are examples of different types of flies the use palmered hackle.

**Parachute**: A style of hackle used on dry fies. The hackle collar is wound on horizontally around the base of the wing, usually a clump wing. A popular form of wing clump around which to wind a parachute hackle is calf-tail hair because of its sturdy texture.

**Proportion**: The design characteristics of various flies that make them resemble the natural they are imitating and perform properly as a fishing fly. Proportion, with most fly tyers, comes with practice. The more you tie, the better your proportions on any given pattern.

**Pulled Down**: Generally, a hackle collar on a wet fly or salmon fly that has all the fibers stroked downward and secured with thread to represent a throat, beard, or legs. However, the top hackle of the collar may be cut off, leaving the bottom to represent the beard style.

## Q

**Quill**: Depending on how it is used, it can mean: the center stem of any feather from which the finer feather fibers (barbs) emanate; the entire flight feather of birds such as ducks, geese, or turkeys; small segments cut from the flight feathers (also called slips); the thin stripped stem from a supple feather, such as peacock quill (used for the body of the Quill Gordon dry), or a portion of the stem of a flight feather, such as Marinaro's Coffin Fly with an extended body made of the pointed end of a quill stem.

**R**

**Rib, Ribbing**: A material used to segment the body of a fly, including thread, floss, oval tinsel, flat tinsel, gold or silver wire, and even dubbed thread. A rib is usually wound in a spiral around the body of the fly.

**S**

**Segmentation**: The construction of a fly body to imitate the defined structure of the natural, especially nymphs, shrimp, and scuds. Segments may be formed with ribbing or through a more involved technique of weaving the body with different colors of floss,chenille, monofilament, or other suitable material.

**Shell**: A material that covers the back of the fly, and is usually used to duplicate the hard, chitonous shell of scuds, shrimp, and other naturals such as crayfish. An example is a shrimp pattern with a plastic sheet pulled over the back of the fly and then segmented with monofilament. Sometimes called a shell-back or over-back.

**Shoulder**: A feather tied in behind the head and extending rearward along the sides of the body for approximately one-third to one-half the body length.

**Spin, Spinning**: Usually this term refers to the technique by which deer hair or similar material is tied to the hook shank and allowed to spin, flare, and rotate around it. This is the technique used to make Muddler Minnow heads, sculpin heads, deer-hair bass bugs, etc. Spin can also refer to the process of twirling a dubbing loop to form a fur-noodle body.

**Spinner**: Refers to the final stage of the mayfly lifecycle in which the insect, after mating and egg laying, lies on the water spent, with its wings outstretched in the surface film. The term also refers to an imitation of this stage, in which the wings are tied in the spent position at right angles to the hook shank.

**Stagger Cut**: A method of trimming excess material in order to form a taper upon which a body may later be constructed. Instead of simply wasting the excess material it is used to perform a function.

**Strip, Stripping**: Usually denotes the removal of barbs from the stem of a feather. It can also mean the removal of the outer sheath of a large quill, such as a goose or turkey quill, which is used to form the abdomen of some nymph patterns, particularly stoneflies.

**T**

**Tag**: The tag is always the rearmost material tied to the hook shank. Tags may be formed of tinsel, floss, or similar wrappings. This term is used primarily in salmon-fly tying.

**Tail, Tailing**: Usually, it is the part of the fly that extends beyond the hook shank. When imitating aquatic insects, it represents the tail of the natural. In streamer flies, however, it is simply a part of the overall construction and does not necessarily represent the tail of the baitifsh.

**Tandem Flies**: A fly in which two hooks are connected by wire or monofilament and materials are tied to both hooks, or materials cover both hooks. This type of fly construction is usually used in large streamer, salmon, or saltwater flies where length is important and a single hook would result in short strikes.

**Tent Shaped or Tenting**: Usually wing material that is tied over the back of a fly in a tent-like shape to imitate the wing of the natural, particularly caddisflies and hoppers.

**Thorax**: The forward portion of an insect's body. This area is much fuller than the abdomen and includes legs, wing case or wings. It also refers to a specific style of dry fly known as a "thorax tie," which has the hackle wrapped around a dubbed thorax.

**Throat**: Similar to a beard, a throat may be made of feather or fur materials and it usually extends along the underside of the shank to the point of the hook. On long-shank hooks throats are usually somewhat shorter.

**Tip**: The second material, after the tag, tied to the rear of the hook. Usually used only in wet or salmon flies and commonly made of floss or wool.

**Topping**: The material tied over a wing of a salmon or streamer fly. For many salmon-fly patterns, a topping of golden-pheasant crest feather is popular.

**Trolling Flies**: Extra large streamer type flies, which are usually tied in tandem (see Tandem Flies) and trolled deep for landlocked salmon and lake trout.

**Tying Silk**: This simply means the tying thread, and is a carryover from earlier days when silk was the standard thread used for fly tying. Unlike some modern threads, silk does not stretch, which is one reason is remains popular with some contemporary tiers.

## U

**Underbody**: A part of the fly tied to the hook shank to add shape or weight to the finished fly . A number of materials can be used to form an underbody, including thread, chenille, floss and lead wire, just to mention a few.

## V

**Variant**: A type of dry fly in which the hackle collar is usually two or more sizes larger than normal, as related to standard dry-fly proportions. The Gray Fox Variant is an example of this type of fly.Variant also refers to a type of rooster neck on which the colors or shadings vary.

The feathers may have varied colored barrings such as on a Red Variant, Cree, or grizzly, or the entire neck may consist of indiscriminate mixing of different color feathers.

## W

**Wing**: The part of a fly that imitates the wing of the natural insect being imitated. Also, the part of a streamer and salmon fly that gives the fly most of its overall shape. With these types of flies, the materials that go over the top of the fly from the head rearward are referred to collectively as a wing.

**Wing Case (Elytron)**: This dorsal structure on a nymph, atop the thorax, contains the developing wings of the adult mayfly.  In fly tying, wing cases are constructed of turkey or duck quill sections as well as a number of synthetic materials

**Wing Pad**: Similar to a wing case, but is tied in behind the eye, extends over the thorax and vibrates freely. Unlike a wing case, it is not tied down at both ends.

**Wing Slats**: Used on caddis pupa imitations to imitate the forming wings emerging from the sides of the thorax.